Higher Education in India and China: Select Perspectives

Higher Education in India and China: Select Perspectives

Edited by

Sreemati Chakrabarti

AAKAR

Higher Education in India and China: Select Perspectives
Edited by Sreemati Chakrabarti

First Published 2018

ISBN 978-93-5002-554-3

Published by
AAKAR BOOKS
28 E Pocket IV, Mayur Vihar Phase I,
Delhi 110 091
aakarbooks@gmail.com
www.aakarbooks.com

Designed by
Limited Colors, Delhi 110 092

Printed at
D.K. Fine Art Press, Delhi 110 052

Contents

Foreword

In 1980, Deng Xiaoping said that China should learn from India in two fields: higher education and modernization of agriculture. Perhaps he had the IITs, IIMs and some prominent universities in mind in the first case and the Green Revolution in the second. Less than four decades later, indeed Indian IT professionals were leading global giants such as Microsoft and Google. But China has gone ahead of India vastly expanding its higher education sector and is fast emerging as a global leader in research. Yet, as this important volume shows, both the countries face major challenges in achieving their shared goals of providing *access* to all wishing and deserving to avail higher education, achieving high *quality* of education with world standards and securing *equity* in society through education. The challenges appear to be formidable especially because the contemporary leaders of India and China have affirmed their goal to make 'innovation' as the main driver of achieving growth of their economies. In that agenda, higher education plays the central role. But as many of the contributors show, access and equity may be sacrificed in pursuit of innovation, excellence and quality.

As the China-related contributions in this volume point out, the role of higher education in the reform agenda in China has remained central right from the beginning of the reforms. The Academy of Social Sciences was carved out as a separate entity from the Academy of Sciences and many specialized Academies were formed thereafter. Key universities were identified for research. State funding to these academies was never meagre. Research was a major input for policy-making by the State agencies. Implementation was seriously examined by research institutes. Researchers were given autonomy to come up with independent views based on their research. Every province had its own Academy of Social Sciences and other sciences. Some of them such as the Shanghai Academy enjoyed no less prestige than the National Academy. Scholars moved to Government positions right up to the high ranks, in one case to the Premier as was the case with Zhu Rongji. In India, the contrast was vivid. Except for two sectors, Atomic Energy and Space, research has not been a priority in the Indian policy making. The original idea of the CSIR (Council for Scientific and Industrial Research) that gave rise to the regional laboratories and research institutes did not get adequate funding in the recent decades. Social Science research was no priority. So the gaps with China continued to grow.

With globalization acquiring momentum and people's demands for basic rights to education and health growing, both India and China faced dilemmas. Policies of the so-called fiscal discipline led to reduction of State allocation of funds for education. But investment was required to promote cutting edge research and innovation. China clearly went in for high investment in key areas and select institutions. India was on its way to do the same thing by declaring ten institutions of national significance. The establishment of more IITs, IIMs and AIIMSes in various states was the beginning of this process. But both countries realized that State funding was not adequate. So they opened their doors to the establishment of private universities. The experience with private universities, as examined by the Indian contributors was not very encouraging. Over 200 private universities in India may have provided enrolment to a large number of students, but the quality of education has suffered. In China too, private institutions have come up. But there seemed to be greater checks on quality control there.

Achieving global standards being the common aim of both the countries, they seemed to pursue the same route but at varying pace. Both had the tradition of missionary colleges and schools during the colonial period. In recent years, China allowed the setting up of local campuses of numerous foreign, especially US, colleges and universities. As one author in this volume points out, internationalization was one of the ways to respond to the new challenges of the neoliberal era. International ranking of educational institutions guided the Chinese perspective. More and more Chinese institutions were moving up in the global ranks. But internationalization had its own problems.

Educational agenda of post-colonial countries was subjected to much debate during the anti-colonial struggle in both India and China. As one author in this volume shows, China had a great tradition of learning. So had India. But colonial experiences and post-colonial educational agenda serving nation-building, nearly disconnected their civilizational traditions from the new educational paradigm. Whatever 'cultural and political' elements were accommodated in the early decades in the curricula of school and college education were later regarded as irrelevant to the agenda of economic growth and technological modernization. The reforms in China and India adopted a new educational agenda derived from the knowledge system guiding the Western Industrial Revolution. Educational institutions and research centres were fully integrated with the western system. That is under scrutiny today. The development path and the knowledge system underlying it are causing crises at many levels producing social inequality, regional disparity, environmental degradation and ethno-cultural alienation. Several papers in this volume dissect that process closely.

I commend this work as an important contribution to the ongoing global discourse on education and development.

Manoranjan Mohanty

Vice-President, Council for Social Development,
Honorary Fellow, Institute of Chinese Studies
and former Professor of Political Science,
University of Delhi

Acknowledgements

The Institute of Chinese Studies, Delhi (ICS) organized a conference on February 27-28, 2015 in New Delhi with the title "'Higher Education in Transformation: Perspectives from India and China". Papers were presented by fifteen scholars from India and China. Some of the papers presented at the conference form the chapters of this book. I wish to express my thanks to the Indian Council for Social Science Research for providing the Institute with a grant to hold the event. The India International Centre, New Delhi, which was the venue of the conference, also provided support for which I am grateful. Some part of the expenses was met from the annual grant provided to the ICS by the Ministry of External Affairs and I am thankful for that. Thanks are due to all the chapter writers who met the deadline that I gave to them. May I also express my gratitude to the then Director of the ICS, Professor Alka Acharya and her staff for the help and cooperation provided in the planning and execution of this conference. The present Director of the ICS, Ambassador Ashok Kantha has also been very supportive of this endeavour. Professor Manoranjan Mohanty, my mentor and teacher, who has written the Foreword to this volume, was the one who insisted on holding this conference and getting a publication out of it. I am greatly indebted to him. Thanks are due to Mr. K.K. Saxena, the publisher, for his efforts and cooperation.

Sreemati Chakrabarti

Introduction

Education and the knowledge created by it have been vitally important tools in the progress of the human society. Educational institutions, existing since time immemorial, have been central to the progress and development of the human race. In the past, institutionalized higher education emerged and developed in the western world first in the form of theological seminaries and later in the form of universities. Oxford and Cambridge in Britain and Harvard and Yale in America became universally acknowledged centres of world scholarship and remain so till date. Historically, in India and China, the importance of higher education was never undermined. India's Nalanda University and China's Academies are illuminating examples. The phenomenal growth of higher education in Europe and America contributed hugely to the western industrialization and technical achievements.

The nineteenth century witnessed the introduction of western education in India and China when Western-style universities and other tertiary institutions were set up in these two countries. This began with the advent and consolidation of colonialism. In China, Jesuits and other Christian missionaries were active in promoting several forms of Western education and in India, which was a direct colony of the British, both the government and Christian organizations set up universities and colleges. The present higher education systems in India as well as in China, by and large, continue to follow the Western model – British in India and American in China. There was an immplicit consensus among the Indian and Chinese elites in the post-Independence and post-Liberation period respectively that the western system of tertiary education had no alternative. However, there were debates regarding certain aspects and features of the system and some of them have been discarded. In the first few decades after India's Independence and China's Liberation almost the entire higher education sector remained under the purview of the Governments or in other words, were public-funded. In India, a substantial number of comprehensive universities, medical and engineering colleges and other technical institutes were set up and this led to significant expansion of the qualified human resources much needed for India's drive for industrialization and growth. In China, in the early post-Liberation years, one sees the near complete Sovietization of tertiary education. Comprehensive universities were drastically reduced in number and a large number of technical or specialized institutes were established. The rationale behind this was that war-torn China's speedy industrialization under the aegis of the Soviet Union was in dire need technical manpower which was at that juncture in short supply.

Although shifts and adjustments in policies related to higher education were taking place in India and China in the early decades it was with globalization and liberalization in the early 1990s that noticeable transformations in the two societies were witnessed. Domestic compulsions in both the countries were also factors which led to this transformation. Put more pointedly, economic globalization and the emergence of the need for a knowledge economy were the two driving forces which brought about the reorientation of higher education systems and institutions the world over. Since the 1990s, large numbers of universities and higher education institutions (HEIs) have reshaped their style of governance, streamlined their functioning and readjusted their priorities. With rapid economic growth, India and China found themselves in a situation where change in the tertiary education system was required in a variety of ways. New challenges of a liberalized economy were evident. To meet these challenges, remarkable transformations in the higher education arena took place. A like—are prioritized over humanities and social sciences. Private higher education existed in pre-Liberation China, but was completely done away with in the Maoist era. It was reintroduced in the reforms period and more so in the 1990s with the advent of the second phase of reforms which were carried out with the adoption of the principle of 'socialist market economy'. Kavita Sharma discusses the contradictions which have resulted with the emergence of a fast-growing private higher education sector in China. She elaborates on the tensions between the private universities and the governments. The governments wants to maintain tight control and the universities demand more autonomy. Private universities are unable to get either quality teachers or quality students leading to these universities being considered as second class. Similar reasons have prompted the Indian State to allow private higher educational institutions to emerge. The Central and state governments are unable to find adequate resources for an expanding higher education sector and that gave way to private higher education particularly in the areas of medicine, engineering, computer science, management and law. Apart from this, higher education institutions add to the disparities already existing in Indian society. They charge high fees and often compromise on quality. However, over a period of time, these institutions may, the author says, "position themselves as high quality/high cost alternatives to mass/low cost public higher education." Privatization of higher education is not limited to setting up of private universities, but even public-funded universities have introduced self-financed courses to generate resources for the universities. Sharma points out that there are four models of private higher education in India. On the whole, it is the role of the governments that will determine the acceptance of private higher education in the country. So far, only contradictory trends are visible. The governments appear to promote private higher education but at the same time attempt to regulate it. A clear-cut policy, therefore, is required.

Saumen Chattopadhyaya and Aishna Sharma are the authors of the third chapter called: 'Higher Education Policy in

India during the Post-Liberalization Era'. Expansion, inclusion and excellence being the major objectives of higher education reforms, the authors explain their possible implications in the higher education scene. This chapter mainly focuses on the issues pertaining to the introduction of the private sector and market-oriented approach towards tertiary education. Reforms in India have taken place in two phases. In the first phase called the 'phase of "endogenous privatization" the focus was more on the reform of government-funded institutions where the mode of funding was to be changed. The Punnaya Committee Report on financing the higher education sector highlighted the need to review and restructure the norms of financing the higher education structure and was debated during this period and so was the Birla-Ambani Report. In the second phase, privatization was highlighted which helped in finding alternative funding and also the role of the State was redefined. In this phase one witnesses a remarkable rise in the number of private universities, from 14 in 2007-08 to 201 in 2009-10. The authors also discuss some of the attempts by the Government to boost private higher education using the Eleventh and the Twelfth Five-Year Plan documents as well as those of the National Knowledge Commission and the University Grants Commission. However, none of the efforts show any overall improvement of the situation as disparities are bound to occur. In a country like India with the wide prevalence of income inequality there is a possibility of exclusion of the meritorious but poor students. The three objectives of expansion, equality and excellence cannot be met by leaving higher education to the vagaries of the market. To begin a transition when India is not ready for the same with disparities in caste, gender and region may be harmful to the education system as a whole.

G. Balatchandirane authors the fourth chapter called 'Higher Education in India and China: Game Changer or Opportunity Lost' looks at the pivotal role that higher education can play in both India and China under the current globalization trends. In any given economy, after a point in time the core economic activity will be defined by the production and consumption of knowledge, where innovation takes precedence over the exploitation of natural resources. Tertiary institutions support growth strategies for knowledge driven economies by training a qualified and an adaptable labour force. In turn, they generate new knowledge and build capacities to access the existing repositories of global knowledge, as well as adapt that knowledge for local use. Balachandirane emphasizes that the cornerstone of a knowledge society is advanced research as well as higher education. He points to the window of opportunity provided by the demographic dividend in these countries and how time is the essence in exploiting it. Further, the existence of a large share of a young population does not automatically lead to higher growth. Higher education, which is a specialized form of human capital, needs to be exploited actively. Secondly, higher education is one vehicle to ensure the formation of an equitable society in the long run. Third, the increasing importance of innovation capabilities in the knowledge economy points to the importance of higher investments in higher education and knowledge creation as well as innovation in these societies. Fourth, no country has been able to become a developed one without substantial investments in higher education. Fifth, given the tremendous externalities that flow from investments in higher education, public provisioning of the same is very important. The strong privatization trends that have been allowed by the passive withdrawal of the State from higher education have to be countered. Leaving things to the market mechanism is a sure recipe for disaster.

Sreemati Chakrabarti's write-up (Chapter V) is devoted to the internationalization of the tertiary education sector of India and China. As obvious from the title: 'The State in the Internationalization of Higher Education: India and China Contrasted', it reveals the marked differences in the policies and actions of the Governments of the two countries in internationalization of higher education particularly in the era of globalization and liberalization. In this era, the meaning of this phrase has expanded from the traditional scenario envisaging an exchange of students and member of faculty and transfer of knowledge to a much more dynamic one involving the projection of soft power of nations as well as commercial and political considerations. Along with expansion and diversification of university education, the Chinese leadership gave a massive push to its drive for internationalization so that its universities reach world standards. One notices a phenomenal rise not only in the number of student and faculty exchanges, but also introduction of new courses, new areas of research and so forth. In China, the aims and goals have a feasible direction whereas in India, although the signs are visible, policies are unstable and do not match the stated intent. The National Higher Education Mission does not possess a concrete plan for internationalization. Also in India's case, the pressures and pulls of a democratic polity have caused the regime to make only half-hearted efforts towards meaningfully internationalizing the higher education sector.

Rui Yang's account which follows is titled: 'Hitting a Glass Ceiling Soon? A Preliminary Assessment of China's Higher Education Development' is the sixth one in this volume. Professor Yang's position is that while China is speedily developing its higher education system to reach international standards, this may not be worthwhile in the long run as this may not be in tune with the Chinese culture. The author says, "Pumping resources into universities will lead to diminishing returns as Chinese culture and practices will act as a brake to the pursuit of academic excellence". He is critical of scholars who only see certain aspects of highly complex issues. A cultural perspective is often lacking in assessing China's higher education development. As universities are cultural institutions and China is rich in higher learning traditions, a cultural perspective is required. Western-style universities may appear to be the norm in China today where academic freedom and financial autonomy are taken for granted. Pointing to China's long unique academic tradition where institutions of higher learning had political utility defined by the ruling class as its central focus, Yang believes, the tradition is in contradiction of the modern university system. Constant tension, therefore, emerges due to this and this affects the efficiency of university operation and China's traditions have become more of a problem than an asset.

'Ethnic Minorities, Integrative Nationalism and Higher Education in Yunnan Province' is written by Ritu Agarwal. China in recent times has witnessed a series of ethnic clashes between Han and ethnic minorities in different parts of the country. The Chinese Government has formulated various preferential policies like quotas in higher education institutions; still the percentage of enrolled students in central universities remained much lower in the case of ethnic minorities. Given this background, the author has examined the case of the Yunnan Province as to how the State has changed its policy of being 'assimilative' to 'accommodative' towards the ethnic minorities. During the Maoist era, the provincial government using some criteria of common language, territory and religion categorized the population into twenty-five ethnic groups. Yet after the reforms, there have been contradictory trends. On the one hand, the State is trying to integrate these minority people by making them adopt the mainstream culture and education, but also on the other hand, keep their ethnic differences intact. It is particularly reflected in the revival of religious education in case of Bai, Dai and Hui minorities in Yunnan. The increasing number of Buddhist temples, cultural and religious festivals and opening of bilingual schools further add to this process of recognizing ethnic minority interests vis-a-vis the State. In fact, this process of recognizing cultural identities helps the State in legitimizing its presence in Yunnan which is home to more than a dozen of minority nationalities in China.

Anamika is the author of the final chapter called: 'Sweden's Contribution to Human rights Education in China and the Raoul Wallenberg Institute'. As is clear from the topic, it is a case study of a Swedish academic institution which deals with human rights education. After the Tiananmen incident of 1989, China's human rights image, which was anyway not impressive, deteriorated even further. Seeing China's long-term economic potential, Sweden along with the European Union set up a long-term dialogue process with China. As part of this discourse, the need for Human Rights Education was spelt out. The Chinese regime saw this more as an opportunity than a threat to its international relations. The Raoul Wallenberg Institute (RWI) was given the responsibility to initiate a two-year master's programme in Beijing University. This was remarkable as the Chinese State was involved in increasing human rights awareness among its people. The challenge, however, was if it would help in the emergence of a human rights culture that permeates throughout Chinese society. Anamika states that a close examination of the courses is not convincing enough to show much promise. The course structure is mainly focussed on legal aspects of international human rights and does not give an opportunity to the students to connect international human rights with the social, cultural and local realities that exist in China. Nonetheless, the programme does have the potential to create an awareness of international human rights standards and principles among those who take up the course but whether it can institutionalize a human rights culture in China would remain questionable. The programme has a limited reach and outcome. However, despite this, the RWI's role in China has been significant as it broke the deadlock between China and the international community in the 1990s. Teachers, researchers and students associated with this initiative have given it a positive assessment.

1

Higher Education in China Has Entered a New Era

Shiyan Lou and Ka Yin Chau

The development of higher education has followed a tortuous path since the foundation of the People's Republic of China (PRC). Public and private higher education institutions (HEIs), with a total number of 205, in Old China were taken over and private institutions were merged into public ones. Chinese higher education progressed steadily according to the plan of the Government under a centralized management system established in 1955. But unfortunately, it was completely destroyed during the period of the 'Great Cultural Revolution', and the cessation of normal enrolment lasted up to six years for most HEIs.

Since 1978, with the implementation of reform and opening-up policy, China has been paying attention to economic development. And the fast-developing economy accompanied by rapid social transformation brought both unprecedented opportunities and great challenges to the development of higher education. On the one hand, the leaders of China began to realize the importance of talents and the Chinese Government started attaching much greater importance to the development of higher education. Deng Xiaoping, an advocate of reform and opening up, said, "Science and technology are primary productive forces." That is to say, science and technology, which in turn depend on talents trained by higher education, play an extremely important role in economic development. And to develop education has become an important part of China's every Five-Year Plan. On the other hand, cultivating talents needed by the rapidly reforming and developing economy and society is not an easy task. It will be more challenging for higher education to "open out towards the world, towards the future and towards modernization" and to "better serve the socialist construction" with professors accustomed to living at HEIs, which were well-known as ivory towers isolated from reality. Moreover, the reform of the education system did not go on without a hitch.

I. The Three Major Phases

Higher education in China has been developed dramatically since 1978, with the rapid expansion of HEIs and the great increase in the number of students. The development of Chinese education lay not only in the expansion of scale, but more importantly, in the ongoing and all-round reform of the system, including the speeding up of internationalization and the occurrence and deepening of marketization. Higher education in China has made unprecedented achievements, of course accompanied by some new problems. The rapid development of higher education is the result of reform and opening up, and in turn promotes the implementation of this policy and the rapid development of economy and society.

Since 1978, the Government has formulated a series of policies and adopted a series of measures, which fundamentally changed the path of higher education and led to the present landscape of Chinese higher education. So far, the development of higher education has completed three major phases: recovery during 1978–85, steady development during 1985–98, and leap-forward during 1999–2009. Presently, the development of higher education has entered a new era of quality education.

The First Phase (1978–1985): The Recovery and Reconstruction of Higher Education

Since the higher education system was totally ruined during the Great Cultural Revolution and higher education became chaotic, it was of great urgency to pay extra attention to the reconstruction of this system. Higher education system actually includes many subsystems, such as the ownership system, the government-management system, the inner-administrative system, the funding system, the enrolment system, the graduate employment system and the academic degree system. During this phase, the higher education system was rebuilt through different methods.

Some of the subsystems existed in the 1950s or so, such as the enrolment system, the government-management system and the administrative system. These recovered with some sort of reform. As for the enrolment system, the Unified National College Entrance Examination (NCEE) was formally resumed in 1977, which was an inspiring event for many people. The government-management system mandated the unified leadership of the Central Government and decentralized management of HEIs at the central and the local levels of government in 1979, making it possible for the local government to actively participate in the running and management of higher education and laid a good foundation for the further expansion of administrative rights of the local government. More and more universities adopted the inner-administrative system of president responsibility under the leadership of the Central Committee of the Communist Party of China (CPC).

Some of the subsystems were reformed or newly established, such as the ownership system, the funding system, the graduate employment system and the academic degree system. The reformed ownership system legally permitted the establishment of private HEIs. The funding system enabled funds for higher education to be provided respectively by the Central and local governments according to the affiliation of HEIs. The graduate employment system changed from "the unified distribution of all college graduates" according to the government plan to a new system implemented in 1985, by which "students apply, HEIs recommend and employers choose". And the academic degree system finally came into existence in 1980.

These reforms were guaranteed by some important government documents or legislation. In September 1979, the report on the re-issuance of the 1963 "Decision on Strengthening the Higher Education System of Unified Leadership and Decentralized Management" was approved by the Central Committee of CPC. The 1982 Constitution of the PRC stipulated that "the state encourages collective economic organizations, state-owned enterprises, public enterprises and social forces to participate in the education enterprise in accordance with the law", which provided a legal basis for the development of private higher education. The promulgation of "The Academic Degree Regulations of the PRC" in 1980 demonstrated the formal establishment of degree system in the PRC.

With the reform of its system, higher education developed rapidly. From 1977 to 1985, the number of HEIs increased from 404 to 1,016, i.e. increased by 151.49 per cent within 8 years. The number of students and teaching staff increased correspondingly, with students from about 625,226 to 1,790,331, with a total increase of 186.35 per cent and an average yearly increase of 10.77 per cent, and full-time teachers from about 190,000 to about 344,000, with an average yearly increase of 7.70 per cent. Number of students per 100,000 population in higher education increased from 66 in 1977 to 161 in 1985. And promotion rate from senior secondary schools to higher education increased from 4.66 per cent to 31.49 per cent. Refer to Appendices Table 1A and 2A.[1] Yet, the gross enrolment rate in 1978 was 1.56 per cent and 3.68 per cent in 1989, which meant that the opportunities for young people to receive higher education were still slim. Moreover, the management of HEIs was highly centralized and the development of private education was slow.

The Second Phase (1985–98): The Stable Development of Higher Education

Although higher education system was reestablished during 1978 to 1985, yet with the deepening of the reform of Chinese social and economic systems and the expansion of higher education, the defects of the highly centralized higher education system became increasingly prominent. Therefore, higher education in China entered a new phase of gradual reform and stable development, which was a typical and important phase of elite higher education.

Reform was also led by the Government and guaranteed by a few documents, such as "Decision on the Reform of the Education System" issued by the CPC Central Committee in 1985, and "Outlines of Educational Reform and Development" (the 1993 "Outline") issued by the Central Government in 1993. And in 1998, China's first higher education law was passed, which determined the directions for the reform and development of Chinese higher education in the twenty-first century.

A significant characteristic of this phase was marketization, which was demonstrated by the following aspects:

Firstly, as for government-management and inner-administrative systems, the power of local governments and the autonomy of HEIs increased. Therefore, on the one hand, local government could administrate HEIs according to local features and demands; and on the other hand it became easier for HEIs to be adapted to the change of the society. In addition to the NCEE, recommendation method of enrolment was adopted since 1988, that is, outstanding students could be admitted by universities without taking part in the NCEE. Policy of "mutual choices between graduates and employers" pattern was formed gradually. And most graduates would choose their own jobs through the labour market. International exchange and cooperation, which was both an independent part and a part of marketization, entered a new stage of fast and normative development.

Secondly, the funding sources became diversified. On the one hand, private HEIs broke the State monopoly. The State has been supporting and standardizing the running of schools by non-governmental sectors since the mid-1980s. During 1992–1994, as many as 406 private HEIs were approved and established. In 1996, funds from social entities and individuals were up to 2.62 billion Yuan. The rapid development of private education is an important indicator of the transformation of higher education in China. On the other hand, tuition fee became an important funding source. Since HEIs started self-financing in mid-1980s, a new funding system was gradually established with national public funds as the main source, and tuition fee, income of school-run industry, social donations and fund raising as supplements. (Refer to Figure 1.1A and Figure 1.2A.) In 1986, some HEIs began to enrol a small number of fee-paying students with lower score-line. And in 1989 at most HEIs, every student had to pay tuition fee and the fee-paying students paid much more, which was known as the 'dual-track' system. And in 1994, this system began to be reformed and all one score-line and same tuition fee levels were adopted for different types of students, which was known as 'merging the track' and was completed in 1997.

During this phase, the number of Chinese HEIs increased slightly from 1,016 in 1985 to 1,022 in 1998, and the major characteristics of HEIs then were merging. And the number of students and teachers in HEIs increased steadily from 1985 to 1998, with 3,607,885 students and 407,253 full-time teachers in 1998, with a respective yearly increase of about 5.94 per cent and 1.30 per cent (See Table 2A). Gross enrolment rate of higher education jumped from about 3.5 per cent in the late 1980s and early 1990s to 4.68 per cent in 1993, and gradually increased to 9.76 per cent in 1998. The number of students studying abroad increased sharply from 4,888 to 17,622, and returned students also increased from 1,424 to 7,379. It is a pity that there were still no data for overseas students in China.

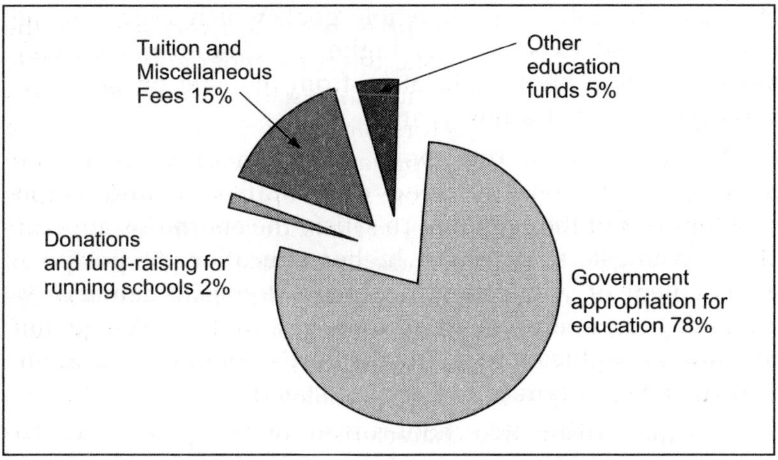

Figure 1.1A: Finding formation in regular HEIs in 1997

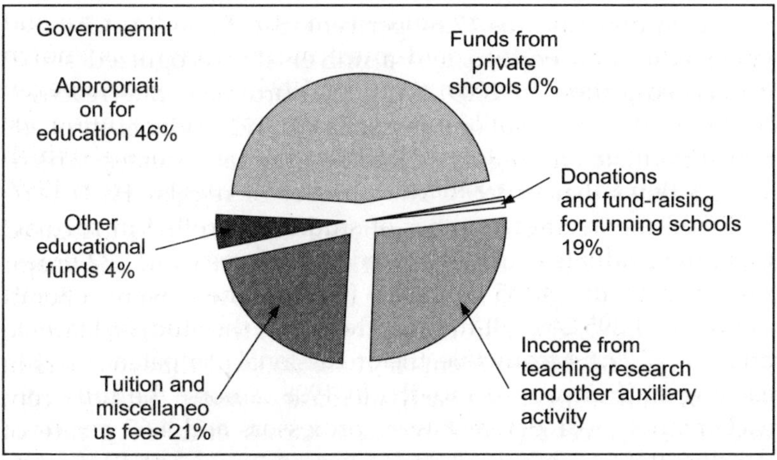

Figure 1.2A: Finding formation in regular HEIs in 2011

The Third Phase (1999–2009): Significant Progress of Higher Education

"Action Plan for Vitalizing Education for the 21st Century" approved by the State Council in January 1999 set massification of higher education as a tangible goal, which triggered the unprecedented expansion of higher education and quickly moved Chinese higher education from the elite phase to the mass phase in just a few years.

The reasons for the above change mainly lay in the purposes to meet the need of sustainable and rapid development of the economy, to satisfy the enormous appetite of the youngsters to receive higher education, to postpone employment of youngsters to expand domestic demand by increasing consumption in education, and to make quality education possible by relieving the burden of basic education, as former Vice Premier Li Lanqing stated.

The most distinctive characteristic of this phase was the rapid expansion. The new enrolments in regular HEIs jumped to 1,640,779 in 1999, with an increase of 41.87 per cent over the preceding year. During this phase, the average yearly increase of new enrolments was 17.64 per cent. See Table 2A. Chinese higher education entered into a universally recognized stage of mass education. In 2009, the gross enrolment rate reached 24.2 per cent, and a total number of 22,851,512 students enrolled in postgraduate and regular full undergraduate courses, which was 5.3 times that of 1998. The number of regular HEIs was 2,305 and the average number of students enrolled in regular full undergraduate courses reached 9,086, increasing 1.72 times compared to the 3,335 in 1998.[2] In 2009, there were a total number of 1,295,248 full-time teachers and the student-teacher ratio was 17.27:1. Meanwhile, the professional competence of the teaching staff improved rapidly. In 1998, among the full-time teachers, only 9.01 per cent were professors and 4.65 per cent had doctorates, while in 2009 the percentages were 10.67 and 13.58 respectively.[3] Internationalization of higher education leaped forward too. Students studying abroad and returned students increased to 229,300 and 108,300 respectively and 117,548 overseas students studied in China in 2009.

Along with the fast development of higher education, a comprehensive reform of higher education system was carried out. The Central and local governments strengthened the role of overall planning, while businesses, organizations, individuals, and international cooperation playing their part in the management of HEIs acting as supplements to the government. Private HEIs became a more important part. HEIs began to raise funds from various channels and self-raised funds of many HEIs surpassed national funding. A more flexible enrolment system, under which HEIs had greater autonomy, was initially established. As for the graduate employment system, a new system of market-oriented independent job choosing had been basically established by 2000. The main task of HEIs became providing such services as job-information-provision and career guidance. These reforms kept pace with the development of higher education and transformation of the society.

II. Social Background of the New Era

Since 2010, when higher education in China entered a new era attention has been paid to quality of teaching instead of quantity expansion. Why was there such a change?

First, higher education in China had been developing fast and the scale was large enough for the present need of the society. On the one hand, as was stated above, the gross enrolment rate was 24.2 per cent in 2009, which meant that China had realized mass education. Moreover, the promotion rate from senior secondary schools to higher education reached 77.63 per cent in 2009,[4] which was a high percentage, namely, more than three quarters of those who intended to receive higher education could be accepted by HEIs. That is to say, the need of the students to receive higher education had been met. On the other hand, most enterprises in China were still labour-intensive, which led to the high demand for manual workers and skilled blue-collar workers and low demand for college graduates who would mostly become white-collar workers. Although education can improve industrial structure by helping to change the labour-intensive enterprises into technology-intensive ones, yet the effect of human capital could not be brought into full use without advanced physical capital and there will be high unemployment rate and waste of talents when the supply of labour far surpasses the demand for it.

Second, with the expansion of higher education and the graduation of more and more students, unemployment of college graduates became a social problem arousing the attention of the Government, the scholars and the public. Generally, the Ministry of Education (MOE) or the State Council would issue documents on promoting graduate employment every year. According to a survey carried out by Institute of Educational Economics Research, Peking University, the immediate graduate employment rate[5] in 2013 was 71.9 per cent and the average initial salary was 3,378 Yuan, which was comparatively low. A lot of scholars studied the unemployment problem of graduates, trying to find out the reasons and the solutions. Presently, there have been about 46,000 papers focusing on this problem, according to the database of CNKI (China National Knowledge Infrastructure).

Third, returns to education began to decline with the expansion of higher education. Most studies on returns to education were specific to urban or rural area since there were great differences between urban and rural areas. Li and Ding (2003) drew the conclusion that the rate of return to any stage of education, including higher education, increased during 1990–1999. Literature review (Lou, 2012) showed that the rate of return to education in China, no matter in rural or urban area, had increased much before 2005. The study of Liu (2013) based on CHNS (China Health and Nutrition Survey) data also showed that the rate of return to education in China increased from 2.77 per cent in 1989 to 10.19 per cent in 2006, while it decreased to 9.78 per cent in 2009. According to supply-demand theory, it is reasonable for higher education to have lower rate of return with the increase in supply of college graduates, which was in agreement with the high unemployment rate of college graduates. Of course, some other factors might also explain this change, such as the financial crisis that occurred in 2008.

In addition to the substantial increase in the number of graduates as a result of expansion of higher education, the reason why employment rate and rate of return to education decreased in recent years also lay in the low quality of education and the imbalance of regional and disciplinary structure. It was a more prominent problem that the quality of higher education was not guaranteed. The major reasons are as follows. The first reason lay in the contrast between the fast-changing society and the nature of education. In a transitional period, the society is changing so rapidly that it is very difficult for education, which is a long-run business, to change in accordance with the outside world. For example, the demand for college graduates from a certain field is changing, but it takes at least four years to have corresponding graduates. Logistics was a case in point. Graduates in this field were badly in need before 2000, but with the rapid expansion of the related programmes, there was surplus several years later. Therefore, the imbalance of disciplinary structure was a major reason why it was difficult for college students to find satisfactory jobs. And it was also difficult to change the ideology, teaching method and lecture content of teachers, especially senior teachers. The backward teaching staff and facilities and out-of-date teaching materials and curricula, which were out of touch with market and social development, provided students with knowledge inapplicable to the future jobs.

The second reason lay in the institution and the system. Although the education system had been changing, it was sometimes lagging behind. To avoid reforming in the wrong direction, it was often the case that with the change of situation, the reform or establishment of a certain system became necessary, which would usually not happen until some pilots showed the workable ways. For instance, College Faculty Congress, as part of administrative system, was formally established in 1985 after six years of trial. It is understandable for the governor and university leaders to be cautious in policy making during the reform period. But lagging behind in institutions resulted in the same problem in practice, leading to the difficulty of the students to meet the need of the society. In addition, as a result of teacher-evaluation system, teachers paid more attention to doing research than improving teaching quality.

The third reason lay in the expansion itself. Firstly, the investment in higher education did not increase in accordance with the growth of enrolment. The expenditure per tertiary student increased form 6,775.19 Yuan in 1998 to 8,542.30 Yuan in 2009, with an average yearly increase of 2.13 per cent,[6] which was much lower than inflation rate. Secondly, the high student-teacher ratio reduced the effort of teachers on each student, making higher education a production line. In the first phase (1978--85) the student-teacher ratio was under 5, and it rose from 5 in 1985 to 11.62 in 1998 at the second phase, and to 17.27 in 2009. Thirdly, the quality of enrolments decreased. In the elite education period, only the best students were chosen to receive higher education, but ordinary even not-so-good students could also be admitted by HEIs in this phase. When the entrants are not so high-quality, it is hard to have high-quality graduates.

With the deterioration of the employment conditions for the new graduates as a result of the rapid expansion of higher education,[7] it became an urgency to change the imbalance of structure and to improve the quality of higher education.

III. The Fourth Era (Post-2010)

The start of this phase was marked by the issue of "The National Plan Outline for Medium and Long-term Education Reform and Development (2010–20)". This document said that China would "take improving the quality as the core task of education reform and development". And the expression of education "quality" appeared forty-eight times in this single document. In order to fulfil this task, a scientific concept of education quality should be established in the first place, for which the criteria should be promoting the all-round development of people and meeting the needs of the society. Universities should be encouraged to have their own characteristics, attracting and cultivating famous teachers and outstanding graduates. The administrative system should be oriented to improving quality of education, and the allocation of educational resources and other works should serve this purpose. National standards for quality of education and the assurance system should be established. The quality of teaching staff should be improved.

As was stated in the 2010 work programmes of the MOE, China would make efforts to improve higher education quality, conduct further "Project of Undergraduate Teaching Quality and Reform" and postgraduate innovation plan, carry out fundamental subjects talent developing plan, strengthen the construction of high-level universities with their own characteristics, perfect quality supervision and guarantee system, perfect academic evaluation mechanism which emphasizes quality and contribution, promote the integration of production, learning, research and application, and improve the capacity of universities for social service. In July 2010, the former president Hu Jintao stressed the importance of education quality in a speech at National Conference on Education.

To improve quality of higher education and employment rate of graduates, the Central Government started to control the growth of enrolments and focus its efforts on improving the quality in 2006. The promotion rate from senior secondary schools to higher education decreased from 2004 to 2007, but the number of new enrolment of college students continued to increase fast.[8] And the increase in the rate of new enrolments has declined since 2010. The yearly increase rate was 2.46 per cent from 2009 to 2013.

In order to provide the talents needed by the rapidly reforming and developing economy and society, teaching quality was paid special attention to. Although student-teacher ratio of regular HEIs was still increasing, yet the speed was much slower, changing from 17.27 in 2009 to 17.53 in 2013. And the quality of teachers was improving fast. For instance, academic qualifications of teachers have improved rapidly.

Among the 1,295,248 full-time teachers in 2009 at regular HEIs, there were 138,161 professors and 360,675 associate professors, the percentages of which were 10.67 and 27.85 respectively. While in 2013, there were totally 1,496,865 full-time teachers, and the percentages of professors and associate professors increased to 12.13 and 28.88 respectively. The educational background of teachers was improving fast, too. In 2009, 13.58 per cent of full-time teachers at regular HEIs had doctorates, and this percentage increased to 19.06 in 2013.[9] Nowadays, it is very difficult or even impossible for one who does not have a doctoral degree to become a teacher in HEIs.

The development of higher education was reflected not only in the slowdown of the increase in numbers but more importantly in the structural and systematic reform.

The structure of higher education changed dramatically. Hierarchically, the percentage of specialized higher education rose substantially. The ratio of regular short-cycle undergraduates, regular undergraduates and postgraduates was 65.91:100:11.10 in 1998, and it became 115.76:100:15.72 in 2006, 96.10:100:15.67 in 2009, and 83.47:100:16.03 in 2013.[10] And compared with regular undergraduates, the enrolment of postgraduates was generally stable, while that of the regular short-cycle undergraduates fluctuated. This change was due to both the adjustment of the HEIs according to the need of the society and the choice of the high school graduates.

As for discipline structure, the proportions of unrealistic or impractical subjects such as literature and of basic theoretical subjects such as philosophy, history and science declined, while those of applied disciplines such as engineering and fine arts and of business-related subjects such as administration increased. For instance, as far as regular undergraduates were concerned, the percentage of literature majors declined from 18.82 per cent in 2009 to 9.9 per cent in 2013, and that of science decreased from 10.18 per cent to 7.2 per cent, while that of administration increased from 16.62 per cent to 18.4 per cent during the corresponding period.[11] The percentage of applied subjects was much higher for short-cycle undergraduates.

With the reform and development in the past phases, an overall higher education system fit for the present development of China has been established. So presently, the major role was to fix some problems and to reform and perfect the system, so as to establish a modern university system. In order to ensure the implementation of educational legislations, regulations and rules, and Educational Supervision Regulations were implemented on October 1, 2012. In September 2014, the State Council issued "Opinions on Deepening the Reform of Entrance Examination", which emphasized the equity of higher education by increasing the enrolment rates of Central and Western China and of the rural areas. In August 2012, the State Council passed "Opinions on Strengthening the Construction of Teaching Staff", focusing on improving the quality and structure of teaching staff, which was the key to improving teaching quality. To fulfil this task, a lot of measures have been taken by the Central and local governments and HEIs, such as financing the teachers to receive more education or to act as visiting scholars at home and abroad. According to the requirement of the MOE, every HEI should formulate its own charter, in accordance with 'Education Law' and 'Higher Education Law', as a normative criterion for the running of their HEI. From November 16, 2013 to October 11, 2014, the charters of 47 universities were approved by the MOE. As a part of establishing modern university system, Regulations on Board of Directors of HEIs were issued on July 16, 2014, which served the purposes of perfecting the administrative system and normalizing the construction of Board of Directors of HEIs. All in all, the systems and practices of Chinese higher education matured with each passing day.

Some new measures have been taken by the Government to improve the quality of higher education and to increase the employment rate of the graduates. China must keep the diversity of higher education to enable graduates to keep their own features. If so, students from different HEIs will face less competition against one another and high employment rates will be ensured. On the one hand, the Central Government helped to improve the creativity of the key universities. "2011

Plan", which was the third national project launched by the State Council following 985 Project and 211 Project, referred to the plan to improve the innovation capability of some universities. According to this Plan, Project 211 universities were promoted to take part in the "985 Project Innovation Platform" and "Characteristic and Key Discipline Project",[12] including cooperative innovation in frontiers of science, culture, industry and regional development. And creativity of HEIs would be improved by innovating cooperation mechanism between production, education and research. On the other hand, the pilot schemes were also started at the Central and provincial levels to convert some universities into applied technical ones.

Meanwhile, with the repeal of the one-child policy in China, the competition (for students) between HEIs is becoming more and more intense. The HEIs are taking measures to strengthen their competitive power. For instance, a lot of local HEIs begin to aim at serving the local economy instead of cultivating top students to serve the nation, which is too high a goal for such HEIs. With this aim, the communication between HEIs and local government, as also local enterprises and local industries is strengthened. Thus, the research of teachers can serve the local economy and students can come to know about the latest developments and obtain the practical skills needed.

IV. Implications and Perspectives

From the above analysis, it can be seen that, higher education in China has undergone dramatic developments and changes in both practice and system since the reform and opening up in 1978 (refer to Figures 1.3A, 1.4A and 1.5A for the overall development). Till now, higher education in China has completed three stages and entered the fourth one. In the first stage, special attention was paid to the establishment of the system, as it was the prerequisite for smooth reform and development. Therefore, many systems were reformed or established and some new policies were made and the development of higher education was not so stable. The second stage was typical of elite education with low enrolment rate and control of scale expansion, and attention was paid to the quality of education. The third stage saw the massification of higher education and large scale increases were achieved. In

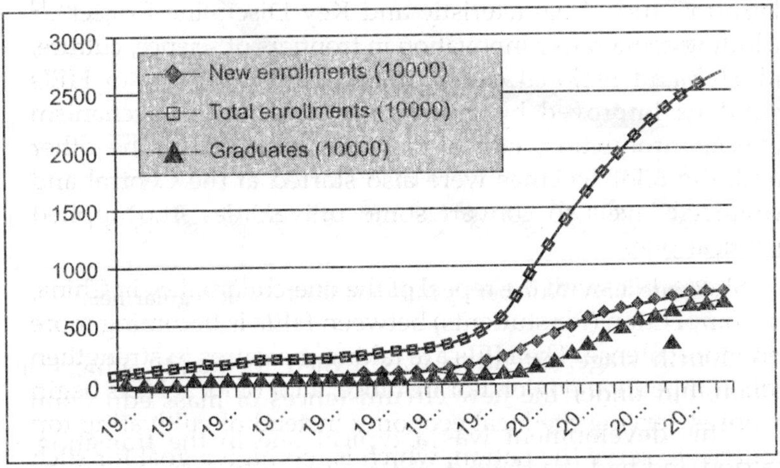

Figure 1.3A: Number of students in regular HEIs

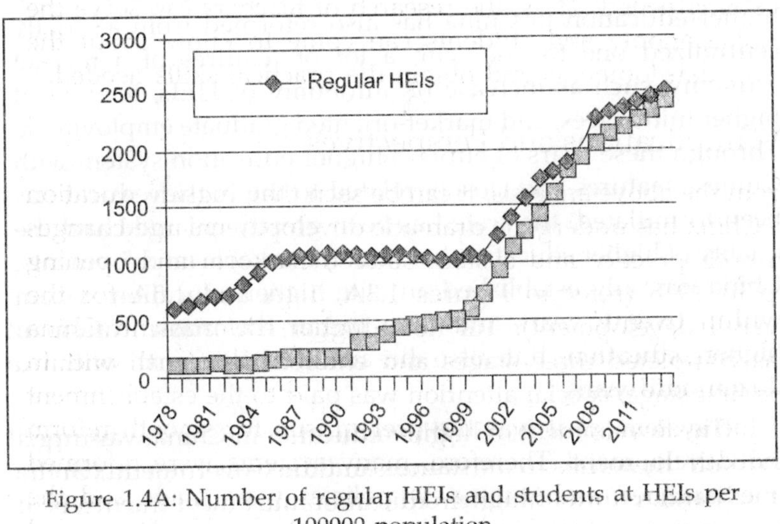

Figure 1.4A: Number of regular HEIs and students at HEIs per 100000 population

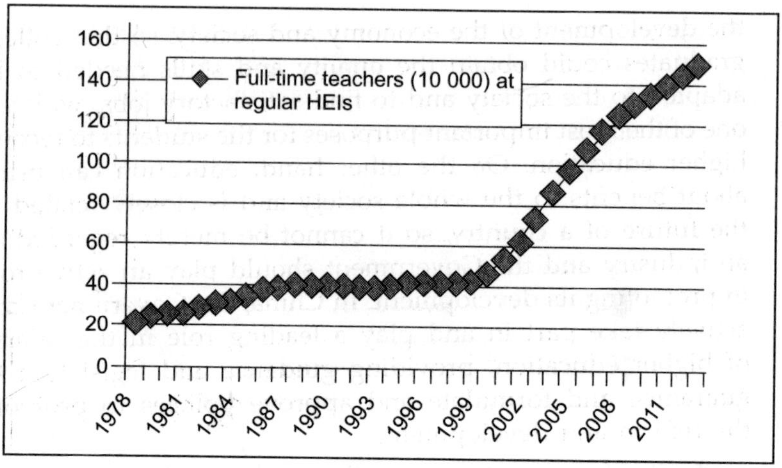

Figure 1.5A: Number of full-time teachers at regular heis

the fourth stage, attention was turned to quality education again, but under the new circumstances of mass education.

This development was a typical one in the transitional period and had the characteristics of transition itself. Chinese economic system has changed from a highly centralized planned economy to a market economy. Correspondingly, higher education in China has also reformed from a strictly centralized one to one with a lot of features of a market economy, such as increase of autonomy of HEIs, levying of higher tuition fees, and market-oriented graduate employment. Through these years of effort, a higher education system with Chinese features and closely related to the outside world has been formulated, the scale has been greatly enlarged and the quality of higher education has seen remarkable improvements. China not only established an elite higher education system within twenty years and then began the massification of higher education, but also she achieved this goal within a dozen odd years.

The development of higher education in China was urged by both the social circumstances and the Government. On the one hand, reform of higher education must meet the needs of the development of the economy and society, so that college graduates could obtain the quality and skills needed to be adapted to the society and to find satisfactory jobs, which is one of the most important purposes for the students to receive higher education. On the other hand, education can bring about benefits to the whole society and is closely related to the future of a country, so it cannot be merely regarded as an industry and the Government should play an active role in promoting its development. In China, the Government did actively take part in and play a leading role in the reform of higher education, providing guidance and legislation to guarantee and formulate and approve policies to promote the reform and development.

In the future, attention will continue to be paid to the quality of education and the quantity of students will not increase much. On the one hand, the Government will not enlarge the scale of higher education rapidly. On the other hand, people are not willing to invest in their own or their children's education if their income will not increase with higher education. To increase the income of college graduates, promoting quality is one of the most important measures.

In order to improve the quality of education, systematic reform will continue to rest the HEIs with full authority so that the HEIs will respond rapidly to market signals according to their own characteristics and advantages. Structural reform will be an important part. No matter what, hierarchy or discipline structure of higher education will be more reasonable and will meet the needs of the society. And marketization of education is the guarantee for this match. The content of lectures and teaching methods will be reformed to meet the need of the society too. Therefore, teachers will be encouraged to cooperate with firms in such aspects as doing research, having part-time jobs, or inviting people with practical experience from enterprises to deliver lectures, and students will be encouraged to obtain internship opportunities, to do part-time jobs, or to take part in teachers' projects. Of course, systematic reform serving this purpose is the prerequisite. For instance, the

Appendix

Table 1A: Data on Development

Indicators	*1977*	*1985*	*1998*	*2009*	*2010*	*2011*	*2012*	*2013*
Number of Regular HEIs	404	1016	1022	2305	2358	2409	2442	2491*
Number of New Enrolments (1000 persons)	273.0	619.0	1156.5	6905.9	7155.73	7375.2	7478.0	7609.7
Number of Total Enrolments (1000 persons)	625.0	1703.0	3607.9	22851.5	23856.4	24730.9	25633.0	26474.7
Number of Graduates (1000 persons)	194.0	316.0	877.1	5682.3	6137.9	6511.6	6733.8	6900.8
Students Studying Abroad (1000 persons)	0.22	4.9	17.62	229.3	284.7	339.7	399.6	413.9
Returned Students (1000 persons)	0.27	1.42	7.38	108.3	134.8	186.2	272.9	353.5
Number of New Enrolment of Overseas Students (1000 persons)	—	—	—	73.27	80.85	94.69	102.99	106.45
Number of Total Enrolment of Overseas Students (1000 persons)	—	—	—	117.55	130.64	147.55	157.85	174.81
Number of Degrees Conferred, Overseas Students (1000 persons)	—	—	—	9.01	11.91	15.20	18.26	19.03

(*Contd.*)

Table 1A: Data on Development (*Contd.*)

Indicators	*1977*	*1985*	*1998*	*2009*	*2010*	*2011*	*2012*	*2013*
Number of Students Per 100000 Population in Higher Education (persons)	66	161	504	2128	2189	2253	2335	2418
Number of Full-time Teachers at Regular HEIs (1000 persons)	190	344	407	1295.25	1343.13	1392.68	1440.29	1496.87
Number of Teachers and Staff in Regular HEIs (1000 persons)	470	871	1029.56	2111.45	2156.6	2204.82	2254.37	2296.26
Percentage of full-time teachers to Teachers and Staff in Regular HEIs (per cent)	40.43	39.49	39.53	61.34	62.28	63.17	63.89	65.19
Student-Teacher Ratio of Regular HEIs (persons)	3.36	5	11.62	17.27	17.33	17.42	17.52	17.53
Promotion Rate from Senior Secondary Schools to Higher Education (per cent)	4.66	31.49	43.05	77.63	83.3	86.51	87.03	87.59

* According to latest data from Ministry of Education (*http://www.moe.gov.cn/*), there were totally 2,542 HEIs, including 2,246 regular HEIs and 296 adult HEIs till July 9, 2014.

Source: *National Bureau of Statistics of People's Republic of China, http://www.stats.gov.cn/.*

Table 2A: Average Yearly Increase Rate of the Four Phases (per cent)

Indicators	*Phase 1*	*Phase 2*	*Phase 3*	*Phase 4 (to 2013)*
Number of Regular HEIs	12.22	0.05	7.67	1.96
Number of New Enrolments	10.77	4.93	17.64	2.46
Number of Total Enrolments	13.35	5.94	18.27	3.75
Number of Graduates	6.29	8.17	18.51	4.98
Students Studying Abroad	47.35	10.36	26.27	15.91
Returned Students	23.06	13.52	27.66	34.41
Number of New Enrolment of Overseas Students	—	—	—	9.79
Number of Total Enrolment of Overseas Students	—	—	—	10.43
Number of Degrees Conferred, Overseas Students	—	—	—	20.55
Number of Students Per 100000 Population in Higher Education	11.79	9.18	13.99	3.25
Number of Full-time Teachers at Regular HEIs	7.70	1.30	11.10	3.68
Number of Teachers and Staff in Regular HEIs	8.02	1.29	6.75	2.12

(*Contd.*)

Table 2A: Average Yearly Increase Rate of the Four Phases (per cent) (*Contd.*)

Indicators	*Phase 1*	*Phase 2*	*Phase 3*	*Phase 4 (to 2013)*
Percentage of full-time teachers to Teachers and Staff in Regular HEIs	–0.29	0.01	4.08	1.53
Student-Teacher Ratio of Regular HEIs	5.09	6.70	3.67	0.37
Promotion Rate from Senior Secondary Schools to Higher Education	26.98	2.43	5.51	3.06

Note: 1. The increase rate was calculated by comparing the number of the end year of a phase with that of the Last Year of the Preceding Phase.

2. Number of new enrolments, number of total enrolments and number of graduates only include data of regular undergraduates and college students, with data of postgraduate students excluded, for there were no such data in 1977.

Source: Calculated based on data from Table 1A.

payment system of teachers should be reformed to encourage teachers to pay more attention to teaching, and experiments in combining teaching with production should be encouraged.

When old problems are solved, new ones always come up. It has to be admitted that higher education in China is still facing a great number of challenges. For instance, with the uneven development of economy and distribution of HEIs, how does the country make higher education opportunities equal for every high school graduate? How to deal with the inequity between public and private HEIs? How to diversify funding channels and increase the percentage of non-government channels without decreasing the enrolment of students from poor families? How to guarantee that HEIs have complete autonomy especially in such aspects as enrolment and internal-administration? And with the increase of autonomy of HEIs, how to avoid corruption in student-enrolment? When reforming personnel system, how to deal with teaching staff of different ages? How to motivate students to study harder? Those problems related to higher education in China are awaiting solutions.

Notes

1. All data are from National Bureau of Statistics of People's Republic of China unless noted.
2. Calculated on the basis of data from "Educational Statistics Bulletin", 1998 and 2009, MOE.
3. Calculated on the basis of data from "Educational Statistics Bulletin", 1998 and 2009, MOE.
4. The percentage rose to 83.5 per cent in 2002 and then was brought down to a lower percentage.
5. The immediate graduate employment rate refers to the percentage of those students who have found their jobs before graduation. Those students who have signed contracts with employers, or who would run their own business, or who have been admitted as postgraduate students or obtained offers from other countries are considered to be employed.
6. Calculated based on data from Statistics Bulletin on Implementation of National Expenditure on Education. 1998 and 2009. Ministry of Education of People's Republic of China. http://www.moe.edu.cn

7. Of course, reasons for that varied, including the structural imbalance and the worldwide financial crisis.
8. The major reason may lie in the baby boom during 1985–1990.
9. Calculated based on the data from MOE. http://www.moe.gov.cn/.
10. Calculated based on the data from MOE. http://www.moe.gov.cn/.
11. Calculated based on the data from MOE. http://www.moe.gov.cn/.
12. In order to give a boost to higher education, the Central Government decided to assign priority to a number of HEIs aiming at building them into world-class universities, which was known as "211 Project" and "985 Project", authorized respectively in 1995 and 1998.

References

Bie, Dunrong and Deguang Yang. *Reform and Development of Higher Education in China: 1978–2008* [M]. Shanghai: Shanghai Education Press, 2009: 2.

Deng, Xiaoping. *Selected Works of Deng Xiaoping* [C], 2nd Edition, Vol. 2. Beijing: People's Publishing House, 1994: 103.

Deng, Xiaoping. *Selected Works of Deng Xiaoping* [C], Vol. 3. Beijing: People's Publishing House, 1993: 35.

Fan Xianzuo. *Mode Selection and Evolution of Chinese Educational System* [M]. Wuhan: Huazhong Normal University Press, 1999: 153.

Li, Lanqing. *Interview with Li Lanqing* [M]. Beijing: People's Education Press, 2003: 119.

Li, Shi and Sai Ding. The Long-term Trend of Rate of Return to Education in Urban China [J]. *Social Sciences in China,* 2003(6): 58–73.

Liu, Jingjing. *Research on the Personal Education Investment Profits and Risks in China* [D]. Weihai (Shandong): Shandong University, 2013.

Lou, Shiyan. *Analysis on Rate of Return to Education and its Influencing Factors in China* [M]. Beijing: Economic Science Press, 2012.

Mao, Lirui and Guanqun Shen. *General History of Chinese Education* [M], Vol. 6. Jinan: Shandong Education Press, 2005: 344.

Ministry of Education of People's Republic of China. Statistics Bulletin on Implementation of National Expenditure on Education. 1998 and 2009. http://www.moe.edu.cn.

MOE. Educational Statistics Bulletin, 2009.

National Bureau of Statistics of China. *http://www.moe.edu.cn.*

Wu Wei. *Reform and Development of Private Education* [M]. Beijing: Educational Science Publishing House, 2002: 43.

Xie, Zuoxu. *Study on the Massification Route of Higher Education in China* [M]. Fuzhou: Fujian Education Press, 2001: 252.

Yang, Dongping. *Annual Report on China's Education, 2014*. Beijing: Social Sciences Academic Press, 2014.

Ying, Wangjiang. *Reform and Development of Higher Education in China*: 1978–2008 [M]. Shanghai: Shanghai University of Finance and Economics Press, 2008: 27.

Yu, Li. *History of Chinese Higher Education* [M], Vol. 2. Shanghai: East China Normal University Press, 1994: 3.

2

Higher Education Policy in India during the Post-Liberalization Era

Saumen Chattopadhyay and Aishna Sharma

1. Introduction

The beginning of the post-liberalization era during the early 1990s in India was marked by the Structural Adjustment Programme (SAP) advocated by the World Bank and the stabilization package advised by the International Monetary Fund (IMF). While the loans from the World Bank sought to foster competitiveness at the sectoral level by encouraging private sector participation in a regulated market, the stabilization package targeted fiscal deficit in terms of GDP to stabilize the macro-economy by reining in the expenditure growth and mobilizing more revenue[1]. In a way, these two sets of measures mutually complement each other as a reduction in fiscal deficit seeks to create more space for the private sector and embracing of the market. Social sector policy reform was also increasingly being framed within the overarching framework of neo-liberalism which informs both SAP and stabilization package[2].

This paper seeks to examine the series of reform measures mooted and implemented for the higher education sector in the context of India after the introduction of the new economic policy in 1991. We begin with an examination of the rationale behind the policy initiatives which are in line with the SAP. We divide the post-liberalization phase into two periods. We discuss and speculate on what would be the possible implications of the policies for the three objectives of higher education, expansion, inclusion and excellence.

2. Rationale Behind Reform Measures

Broadly speaking, the entire package of reform measures seeks to construct a regulated market to foster competitiveness so as to reap the benefits of allocative efficiency. Construction of a regulated market entails provision of freedom to the providers as well as to the students who are viewed as consumers, changing thereby the role of the State to only regulator or to the 'facilitator' of the market conditions. The various kinds of freedom to the providers and the consumers which are required to instal market-like conditions can be summed up as in the table below (Table 1).

Table 1: Eight Conditions for Market

'Four freedoms' for providers	*'Four freedoms' for consumers*
Freedom of entry	Freedom to choose provider
Freedom to specify products	Freedom to choose product
Freedom to use available resources	Adequate information on prices and quality
Freedom to determine prices	Direct and cost-covering prices paid

Source: Adapted from Jongbloed (2004).

Market requires that both the consumers and the producers respond to the signals in terms of the prices and the composition of demand.

Four Freedoms for Providers

Freedom of entry. It is assumed that education providers must be given freedom to enter the market for higher education to infuse competition.

Freedom to specify products. The HEIs are given the freedom to design their own curricula and introduce more job-oriented courses, in order to cater to the needs of the students who are amongst the potential contributors to the funds.

Freedom to use available resources. Though education is not for business in India, roping in the private sector would require that not only are they allowed to make 'reasonable surplus' but also to decide on its use[3]. Otherwise, the very driving force for the producers would be conspicuously absent.

Freedom to determine prices. The HEIs must have the freedom to determine the price for the product they sell as they are required to fend for themselves (as government curtails grants). However, the exercise of this freedom has the potential to interfere with the choice making by the students, adding to the exclusivity of the expansionary process.

Four Freedoms for Consumers

Freedom to choose provider and freedom to choose product. Students, as consumers, are to be provided with the freedom to choose not only the institution they would like to seek admission to but also the freedom to choose the courses (credits) they would like to pursue. In a way, the HEIs will now have to face the competition to improve their quality and respond to the emerging nature of demand.

(Note: The first two freedoms (page 50 refers) of choosing the provider and choosing the product have been combined herein.)

Adequate information on prices and quality. The students are provided information regarding the course-wise price in the institution brochure and also with the information on the ranking of HEIs as a guide to the relative quality of HEIs. It is assumed that these two measures would be sufficient for students to make the right choice just like any other market[4].

Direct and cost recovering prices paid. Following the World Bank argument, students should be charged high prices for their education because the students get higher returns in terms of future income streams and thereby the role of prices in generating signals would be restored[5]. This would be efficient and financially viable from the point of view of a private HEI.

The other component of reform is to improve governance to ensure efficiency in resource use at the institutional level and impart good quality education. The governance reform is in line with the new public management (NPM) and public-private partnerships (PPP). Under the NPM as well as PPP, public HEIs are governed in the corporate style to make them efficient and productive. Both seek to improve quality of HEIs as well as the saving of government resources.

Starting from the early 1990s, the entire reform phase can be categorized into two periods on the basis of the intensity with which such measures were proposed and the nature and quantum of shift in the nature of higher education regulation. The second phase saw a greater orientation towards the establishment of a market for higher education than the first, a greater role for the private sector and major initiatives in governance reform. As we shall discuss subsequently, such a paradigmatic shift, with a growing role for the private sector, has serious ramifications for all the three objectives, expansion, inclusion and excellence.

3. First Phase of Reform

India has the second largest higher education system in the world. Its total enrolment stands at 29.6 million, with 633 universities in all during 2012–13 (GOI, 2014). The gross enrolment rate has shown steady increase over the years standing at around 21.1 per cent (ibid.) of the relevant age group at present. The public expenditure on higher education in terms of GDP has barely crossed 1 per cent. But in real terms and in terms of per capita, the rise has been insignificant.

During the early 1990s, there was a cut in the public expenditure for the universities. The plan and non-plan expenditure registered a decline in real terms from 1990–91 to 1995–96, with expenditure on higher education as a percentage of GDP hovering around 0.4 per cent (on an average) from 1990–91 to 2000–01 (Tilak, 2004). This reduction was mostly felt in the maintenance grants, which are required by the universities to support their recurring expenditures, including teachers' salaries. That the higher education was relegated as compared to school level education can be seen by the fact that the share of expenditure on higher education as a percentage of total expenditure on education was only 11.5 per cent, on an average, during the same period (ibid.). It was also a period when the White Paper (GOI, 1997) on government subsidies branded higher education as a non-merit good which was used as a justification for compression of government subsidies. Below we discuss the reform measures suggested by the governments as articulated in the Five Year Plans (FYP), government documents and reports and commissions set up for the purpose of reform of the higher education sector need to be understood within the broad framework for reform strategy as discussed above. The annual growth rates of the HEIs and the enrolment during 1995–96 to 2005–06 were 7 to 8 per cent and 8 per cent respectively (Duraisamy and Duraisamy, 2015).

Public Providers: Funding and Governance

The Punnayya Committee Report (1992–93) (GOI, 1993) argued that central universities should supplement the State's efforts by raising their own resources and thus stabilize their function and development. It suggested that the universities should abhor the negotiated mode of funding[6], because that did not promote internal efficiency and quality. It was proposed that the central universities shift to a mix of input-funding and student funding system. This was argued to be promoting cost efficiency and competition amongst the universities.

The main objective of the Tenth FYP (2002–07) (GOI, 2008) was to raise the gross enrolment ratio from 6 per cent to 10 per cent by the end of the Plan period. The other objectives included increasing access, improvement in the quality through revision of course curriculum and adoption of IT.

The CABE Committee (2004–05) (GOI, 2005) contended that universities should have the freedom to bring in entrepreneurial education and self-financed and job-oriented courses and to look for alternative sources of funding higher education, which would incentivize them to perform better. The level of funding should be enhanced by charging high and differentiated fees, to cover the cost of provision to create some reasonable surplus. The Committee noted that financial aid acted as a tool to curtail freedom of the providers, both academic as well as financial. Thus there was a focus on improving the governance of the public funded institutions and on being more responsive to the demand through changes in the mode of funding. The Committee also suggested to set up an Internal Quality Assessment Cell (IQAC) to ensure quality improvement.

Private Providers

The number of private providers in the first phase was very few. However, the Tenth FYP gave an indication towards increased private participation in the management of colleges and the deemed to be universities, with the two key words of liberalization and internationalization of higher education constituting the overall thrust of education policy reform. The period could be characterized by laissez faireism, in the absence of any government intervention as well as the implementation of a concrete policy regarding the role of the private sector, as argued by Tilak (2014).

Students' Sovereignty

The Punnaya Committee (GOI, 1993) suggested funding via cash support to the students as a part of this approach. The CABE Committee (GOI, 2005) recommended choice-based credit courses which would bring in flexibility in the academic structure besides promoting students' mobility both within the country and abroad, thus ensuring academic parity with international standards. Though educational loans were made available for the students, the demand was low. During 1990–91 to 1999–2001, the annual growth rate in the loans accounts was 5.5 per cent with a growth rate in outstanding loans amounting to 23.8 per cent (Duraisamy and Duraisamy, 2015).

Construction of Market

Despite the limited size of the private sector, the focus was on applying of market principles. To make the system behave more like any other market, the Punnaya Committee recommended instituting certain performance indicators for inter-university comparability (or competition).

The Birla-Ambani Report (GOI, 2000) on reforms in education, also suggested a market oriented competitive environment for higher education institutions. It proposed that funds be reallocated to primary education and user-pay principle must be applied in case of higher education, supported by loan provision. Basically, the Report argued for treating higher education more as a private good and creating a level playing field for larger private sector participation without giving any specific directions for the extent of regulation the market would need. There was opposition to the role of the private sector and the stage was not set for ushering in the market, albeit quasi-market in the context of higher education with adequate safeguards.

During the first phase of reform, the focus was more on the reform of the government funded institutions which was to be spurred by changes in the mode of funding. It can, thus, be called as a phase of endogeneous privatization[7] (Ball and Youdell, 2007). This was also a pre-requisite for making the public universities ready to participate in the market and compete with the private bodies in due course of time and to give freedom to the students. Only with the emergence of a strong and credible private sector in higher education, the government could start veering towards the construction of the market as we would see in the second phase, when the market wave hit higher education in a big way. The presence of the private sector was rather small during the 1990s.

4. Second Phase of Reform

During this phase, the share of public expenditure on higher education in GDP showed only a marginal improvement, at

0.83 during 2007–08 to 2010–11 (MHRD, 2012)[8]. This may be attributed to an increase in the number of public funded universities[9] from 253 in 2007–08 to 308 in 2010–11[10]. At the same time, the average share of school level education in GDP for the same period was higher at 2.31 per cent. The annual growth rate of the HEIs and the enrolment rate were higher compared to the first period at 13 per cent and 14 per cent respectively during 2005–06 to 2010–11 (Duraisamy and Duraisamy 2015).

In addition, this phase witnessed a sharp rise in the state private universities. The number went up from 14 in 2007–08 to 201 (as on 23.02.2015), with a sudden shoot up in the year 2009–10 (Table 2). The private aided and private unaided colleges and universities would now account for 73 per cent of all the HEIs with a share of enrolment touching 62 per cent.

Table 2: Number of State Private Universities over years

Year	*Number of State Private Universities*
2007–08	14
2008–09	21
2009–10	60
2010–11	80
2011–12	111
As on 23.02.2015	201

Source: UGC Annual Report, Various Years

The cost recovery by the public HEIs went up to nearly 40 per cent (CABE), partly contributed by the self-financing courses, rise in tuition fees and other incomes (GOI, 2005).

Providers: Mode of Funding and Governance

The Eleventh FYP clearly spelt out the three major objectives of higher education reform: expansion, inclusion and excellence. The budgetary provision was raised significantly with a larger role for the Government to achieve all the three without there being any trade-off between them. To mitigate the adverse impact on inclusiveness because of rising private participation, scholarship was to be largely relied upon. The Eleventh FYP vision document, however, sought to make it clear that public sector based expansion could deliver on inclusive expansion if corrective measures are adopted to improve quality. Setting up of central universities in all the states was proposed. The Eleventh FYP budgeted for a massive rise of around 4.6 times in its budgetary allocation in comparison with the Tenth FYP.

With respect to the mode of funding, the Eleventh FYP said that Government must see that fee levels are not profiteering and beyond this the State should not interfere in institutional governance (GOI, 2008). The plan therefore did not question setting up fees at levels which meet the costs. Further, arguing for financial autonomy of universities, it posited:

> "Financial Autonomy will enable institutions to mobilize resources from user fees, review fee structures, consultancy services, and donations. They can rationalize their fee structures according to the degree of excellence achieved both in terms of academic achievement and market value. It will also unshackle the institutions, enabling them to take bold initiatives regarding campus accretions/additions, starting new faculties and new disciplines, creating competencies in new knowledge domains, expanding infrastructure, and enlarging student outreach." (*Eleventh FYP*, Vol. 2, pp. 25–26,)
>
> Since most university students come from the top 10 per cent of the population by income levels, they would be able to pay fees amounting up to 20 per cent of the operating cost of general university education. The fees for professional courses could be much higher. (*Eleventh FYP*, Vol. 2. p. 48)

Thus there was emphasis on rendering financial autonomy to the providers to raise their own resources, raise fees, and design their own product.

In order to meet the need for an expansion in HEIs, the National Knowledge Commission (NKC) (GOI, 2009) recommended that the funding should be enhanced from both the public and the private modes. It recommended that the HEIs should look for alternative sources of funding. For this purpose, it was suggested that universities use their lands as a source of revenue, fees be raised to cover at least 20 per cent of the total expenditure, HEIs be allowed to invest in the financial instruments of their choice and use the income from endowments to build up their corpus, universities rope in professional firms to raise resources and so on.

There was apparently a clash of ideas towards higher education reform between the Eleventh FYP and the NKC. While the Eleventh FYP favoured a larger role for the public funding in achieving the higher education objectives, NKC showed enough inclination for a larger role for the private sector. The other major contention was the role of UGC in the emerging context and installation of a regulatory body. Possibly to negotiate between the pro-public sector role in the Eleventh FYP and pro-market pro-private sector role as envisaged in the Eleventh FYP, the Central Government set up the Yashpal Committee for reinvigorating the higher education system. The Yashpal Committee Report sought to reverse the trends of fragmentation and compartmentalization in the system of knowledge generation and knowledge dissemination and suggested setting up of research networks for fostering collaborations. Further, the Report argued for a restructuring of universities on the principle of providing complete autonomy, which is linked with sources of finance, legal framework as also the overall culture under which the university is operating. And therefore universities should be freed from the control of both the Government and the profit making private agencies. It also argued that universities must respond to external environment and must appoint professional fundraisers who have the skills to identify the unique selling points of the university and persuade the potential donors and investors to invest in the university.

The Twelfth FYP in a similar light shows an inclination towards the private higher education while maximizing the output of access, equity and quality, meeting the international benchmarks. It highlights a need for a changed governance system, with new management techniques. The organization of universities should be flexible to meet the needs of a changing society. To effect such a change, the role of the State had to be redefined to that of providing reasonable funding to universities and supporting innovation and development of higher education. The fee structure was suggested to be revised by at least 10 per cent for every 3–year period. As a measure to enhance inclusion in private self-financing institutions, voucher system was recommended to meet the financial needs of the students from the marginalized group. This is a step to enhance the choice at the hands of the students and thereby create competition amongst HEIs (GOI, 2013). However, there emerge two concerns with regard to vouchers, (a) the students suffer from lack of information on the quality of course or institute, making them vulnerable to wrong or poor decision making, (b) the voucher system will infuse the demand driven mechanism wherein the institutes of higher education would compete with each other to cater to a larger share of the market. The nature of this competition may cause institutes to cut down expenditure on academic activities in lieu of on wasteful expenditures like advertisement, having strong implications on their quality of education, or alternatively, they may generate resources.

The Twelfth FYP advocated strongly the public-private partnership (PPP) in higher education, for setting up new universities and colleges and for creating quality infrastructure and physical facilities in the existing colleges. Under this system, the investment is shared in varying degrees between the public and private sectors with respect to management of the HEIs and their infrastructure. Further, it recommended models for industry-institute interface whereby large education hubs be created and the land and other essentials be provided by the state government concerned (ibid.).

The Rashtriya Uchchatar Shiksha Abhiyan (RUSA) (GOI, 2013) also sought to create competition amongst HEIs by recommending performance-based funding of the state universities. It recommended financial as well as academic autonomy for the state universities in order to improve their present deteriorating status. For rendering financial autonomy, the RUSA suggested that every state should set up its State Higher Education Council (SHEC), which would disburse funds to the state universities. Also the Committee suggested that by providing freedom to the state universities, they would enhance their quality. And improving quality was thought to be very vital for its 'demographic dividend' to compete in the global market.

It remains to be seen how many state universities, already suffering from resource crunch, can compete with other national universities or meet the international benchmarks: only a top few, which are reputed and are liberally funded by the state governments would be able to compete. The prevailing hierarchy in the Indian higher education is likely to remain entrenched.

Providers: The Private Sector

The NKC argued that private investment in education should be encouraged. For this purpose, public resources like land should be leveraged especially in the form of land grants to attract more private investment. It also recommended that 1,500 new universities be set up, which would be accorded autonomy to set student fees levels and tap other sources for generating funds. These new universities should form strong linkages with industry.

As mentioned earlier, the Twelfth FYP had argued for the larger role private sector in raising the GER to 30 per cent by 2020. The resources required are five times the current expenditure. The private sector has to emerge as a massive investor particularly in the professional and technical education to achieve the envisaged expansion. In 2012, the Narayana Murthy Committee (GOI, 2012) came up with the suggestion of bringing in greater private sector participation in higher education; it suggested a university-corporate link up in order to enhance the relevance of education and as also to explore an alternative mode of funding research in the universities. RUSA similarly supported the private sector, suggesting that the private universities would also be brought under the purview of funding as long as SHEC approves their role and objectives. This would supposedly reduce state intervention.

The State has proposed a recent initiative of instituting the New Education Policy by the end of 2015. The State sought the views of people under varying themes devised for higher education[11]. Some of the themes clearly articulated the inclination towards encouraging private providers or foreign providers, orienting the existing universities to attract foreign students. Under the theme of quality of regulation, it has been asked how the private providers can be encouraged. Such measures, if initiated, without adequate regulatory measures would only accentuate exclusion with no guarantee for quality education and research.

For the Students

On the consumer side, the Eleventh FYP argued that the students should be charged higher fees for professional courses, because such courses would render them employable in the labour market. It also advocated that those who could not afford be provided with loan schemes by the government.

The NKC discussed about flexibility for earning credits to provide students with more choice. The students have the freedom to assess and choose between universities, bringing in another element of competition amongst the universities. The universities were better made accountable to the students than being overcontrolled by the State (GOI, 2009).

More recently, the UGC has recommended a Choice Based Credit System (CBCS) from July 2015, allowing students to transfer their credits amongst universities recognized by the UGC. This was also suggested in the RUSA (GOI, 2013). This would give a boost to student mobility and expand student choice to let them have their way in such a system. It is assumed here that by responding to the demands of students, the teachers would produce of the best of their efforts. But in view of the variations in the infrastructure facilities, information asymmetry that the students suffer and the very fact that the students are the inputs as well as the customers, it is doubtful whether the proposed system will deliver results. The present system allows for students' freedom to choose courses albeit restricted within the institutions. This is a pre-requisite for the mobility of students across the courses and the institutions to foster competition.

It is to be noted that private expenditure by the students increased during this period as compared to the earlier periods, with the demand for educational loans witnessing substantial growth during 2001–02 to 2012–13. The percentage growth rates in the loans accounts were 31.1 per cent and 39.3 per cent for in outstanding loans account. Educational loan is unlikely to be a panacea for the students because of potential discriminations in terms of courses, gender, income and other hidden characteristics. As of now, only around 9 of 30 million students have opted for loans.

Supply of Skills

In addition to all this, the Eleventh Plan sought to address the deficiency of skilled manpower in the labour market by introducing the National Skill Development Mission. The goal was to create skilled and employable personnel in line with the requirement of the economy. It aimed at generating 500 million skilled people by 2022. This was to ensure that the supply-side responses are perpetually in sync with the demand side impulses both from domestic as well as global economies and therefore both private and public sectors need to be involved via a public-private partnership (PPP) mode. Two Bills were introduced in the Parliament to set up eight new IITs and five new Indian Institutes of Science Education and Research (IISER). A scheme was also prepared to set up colleges in 374 educationally backward districts with lower than the average GER for India.

The integration of skill development with the conventional education has also been proposed by the State under the

'Minimum course curriculum for undergraduate courses under choice based credit system'[12]. This would confine the learning of students to getting trained in certain skills only, in order to become employable.

Construction of a Regulated Market

The National Knowledge Commission (GOI, 2009) argued for the formation of an Independent Regulatory Authority of Higher Education, which would be an overarching body, under which all the bodies would be subsumed. A single body would lead to hassle-free establishment of HEIs, particularly private. Thus, there were indications clear enough towards implementation of a full-fledged neoliberal reform agenda. It was also felt by the NKC that all the three objectives of expansion, inclusion and excellence cannot be pursued unless the private sector is brought in keeping in view the poor governance of the publicly funded institutions.

But the idea of a regulatory body to oversee the entire higher education system and ward off political intervention and confusions arising out of overlapping jurisdictions continued to be considered as a very important policy measure by the policy-makers which primarily led to the formation of a committee headed by Prof. Yashpal. The Yashpal Committee (GOI, 2009) called for a change in the entire governance structure of universities by having an overarching body called National Commission of Higher Education and Research (NCHER) which can be construed to be very similar to what the NKC proposed in the form of IRAHE.

The objectives stated in the NCHER Draft Bill have a clear inclination towards the private-oriented approach. It includes establishing robust global connectivity, making universities globally competitive and connecting universities with industry to promote innovations. For this, the universities would provide practical subjects and therefore justify themselves for charging high fees.

The introduction of a spate of Bills in the Parliament in 2010 was another effort to bring in market-like conditions in higher education. The supposed purpose of the Bills was to infuse more regulation in the system but, there is a need to understand the nature of this regulation. The underlying rationale behind the Bills recognized education and in particular higher education as intrinsically to be suffering from information asymmetry, vulnerability of the process of delivering education to abuse, and irreversibility of educational choices. All these factors lead to market failure, which are sought to be addressed by the Bills. The Bills introduced are the Foreign Education Institutions (Regulation of Entry and Operations) Bill, Bill on prohibition of Unfair Trade Practices, Educational Tribunals Bill, Universities for Innovations Bill, National Accreditation Regulatory Authority for Higher Education Institutions Bill and National Commission for Higher Education and Research Bill.

But the competition the Bills seek to promote would be amongst the unequals and might accentuate the prevailing hierarchy and dualism in the higher education sector, and worsen the loose framework of regulations particularly for the agricultural institutes and for innovation universities, rather than addressing the issue of quality (Tilak, 2010). The Unfair Trade Practices Bill may not address the issue of low quality provided even at high costs (Sharma, 2010). Establishing an overarching NCHER would expedite setting up of private universities, without having to seek permission from the plethora of regulatory bodies (Abrol, 2010; Sharma, 2010). They may not help address all the three major objectives of expansion, inclusion and excellence simultaneously in the wake of rising participation of the private providers (Chattopadhyay, 2012).

Another step to infuse a sense of competition amongst universities is setting up of the National Assessment and Accreditation Council (NAAC) (in 1994), and the UGC has made it mandatory for universities to get themselves accredited to ensure quality education. Also in order to get funding from the UGC under the College with Potential Excellence scheme, the universities must submit an accreditation certificate with a minimum 'B' grade. Acquiring accreditation would also supposedly provide an international recognition to the Indian universities (GOI, 2013). The funding has been made contingent upon the relative performance of the universities.

Further on, in 2010, to monitor the output of teachers in higher education institutions, the UGC advocated minimum qualifications for appointment of teachers and other academic staff in universities and colleges by way of Performance Based Appraisal Scheme (PBAS) (GOI, 2010). The supposed aim is to ensure that the teachers deliver output in return for the salary they receive from the state. Ones who fail to perform are excluded from the so-called market for higher education. Also in the process, the teachers are supposed to be evaluated by the students, the so-called customers of the service providers. This is again a step to render consumer sovereignty to the students and infuse competition amongst teachers/universities to raise their academic standards.

Another step taken to supposedly enhance the quality of education across universities is the inter-university mobility of faculty which was discussed in the Central Universities Bill, 2009 and re-iterated in the Central Universities Bill, 2013. This is expected to alleviate the faculty shortage, broadly speaking, and more importantly in the specific areas of specializations. But given the diversity in the academe, the prevailing system does allow for mobility to respond to specific needs of the institutions through collaborations and mutual exchanges. It is apprehended that a centralized system would actually circumscribe the autonomy of the universities.

Of late it has been recommended in the policy circles to replace the UGC with a National Commission of Higher Education Authority. It was because of UGC's regulatory intervention on the privatization of higher education. And secondly, UGC was found ineffective to deal with global knowledge economy requirements of innovativeness and excellence. This was another attempt to bring in corporate kind of management into higher education and to make profits out of commercializing higher education output globally (Gurukkal, 2015).

The second phase can be named as the phase of endogenous as well as exogenous privatization[13] (Ball and Youdell, 2007) because the Government aims to realize expansion of higher education by a) bringing in the financial form of privatization of public HEI through fees, student loans, self- financed courses and also b) by both active involvement of the private sector and through different modes of partnership between public-private partnership (Tilak, 2012; Tilak 2014).

5. The Rationale of Efficiency: A Critical Review

Very conveniently, the present scenario assumes that by providing the above freedoms to the student as well as the provider, they can exercise their choices and ultimately reach an equilibrium ensuring equality between demand and supply. This arrangement seeks to bring in efficiency.

On account of the requirement to comply with the FRBM Act, both the Centre and the state governments resorted to a cut in the public expenditure, which happened in the 1990s and thereafter though the budgetary allocations. The allotments witnessed a rise during the Eleventh FYP. In relative terms, there has been a shift in the budgeted expenditure away from higher education to the school level, particularly primary level. Allocative efficiency has been stressed upon by the World Bank by emphasizing that the primary level education leads to greater externality than higher education and therefore there should be a shift of resources towards other avenues which give more returns to the economy and we should leave the higher education sector in the hands of private sector. The introduction of the private sector by the way of various bills and public private partnership is a step to bring in this kind of allocative efficiency in the system. In addition to this, the HEIs must justify the funds that they get from the State and to ensure accountability for using these funds, they must deliver certain quantifiable outputs. For instance, PBAS had been introduced and accreditation has become compulsory so that HEIs deliver output and achieve excellence. One fundamental issue with PBAS is that it assumes the relationship between the time spent and the research output as linear. In creative endeavours like these, time spent is rather a futile measurement of quality (Das and Chattopadhyay, 2014).

6. Policy Implications

Freedom for Producers

It needs to be seen how and to what extent neo-liberal conditions for producer sovereignty can be applied to the higher education sector (Chattopadhyay, 2009; Chattopadhyay, 2012). Firstly, if there is any consideration for the quality of higher education, the providers cannot be allowed to gain a 'free entry' to the so called 'market'. The fact that the foreign HEIs and private HEIs would enter the economy is no guarantee that the quality would also be ensured. Second, if the HEIs are given the freedom to specify products, the market-oriented professional courses which are in demand owing to job prospects will be offered. The other conventional courses like arts or literature will never see the light of day. Those students who cannot afford would be excluded from the market. With respect to freedom to determine price, the professional courses may be priced more, leaving meritorious students from economically deprived sections out of the system. Thirdly, giving them freedom to use available resources may lead to misuse of those resources on non-academic activities (ibid.).

Freedom for Consumers

The condition of giving freedom to the students to choose their provider ignores the point that this freedom depends upon the command a student has over resources and their 'market capacities'. Due to this, the condition of cost-determined prices being paid by the students would fail to work. In a country like India, with wide prevalence of income inequality it would mean mass exclusion of meritorious but poor students. This would severely affect the quality because students are the output as well as the important inputs in the system of higher education. Furthermore, while exercising choice, a general course offered by even a topmost institution may not be preferred by students over a professional course offered by any other institutions. This phenomenon also partly leads to the spawning of private institutions, of even little repute. In addition to this, because of the experience of good feelings about higher education, the students can never have complete information about its quality (ibid.)[14].

In addition to the above arguments, incorporating market-like principles in higher education ignores the significance of autonomy within an HEI. In the case of a pure private good, autonomy is always an underlying condition (or assumption) and the economic agents there are not worried much about it. In contrast, the question of autonomy, whether financial, academic or administrative, assumes a vital component in an HEI if it is to fulfil its objectives[15]. The question of autonomy is related to the internal life of an institution. Treating higher education as a private commodity often takes away the autonomy of HEIs because their needs get tuned in with the needs of the markets only. The neo-liberals ignore the true role of education and a university in the society in the context of India.

Market for Higher Education

The higher education policy aims at achieving three objectives of equity, excellence and expansion as discussed above. However, by leaving higher education to the vagaries of the market, it is unlikely that these objectives would be met.

The market for higher education fails on many counts. Higher education is best considered as a quasi-public good as it generates externalities. The propensity of the private HEIs to resort to commercial practices leads to subversion of the educational process and therefore poor quality. The very fact that good quality education is co-produced in the class room with the active participation of the teachers and the students implies that students are not to be treated as consumers. Further, good quality education and research depend on good quality students and teachers who are not reproducible and also on the research environment that prevails. The students are often appeased by teachers through 'high grades' because their promotion depends also upon students who evaluate their performances. Also the better the ranks of the students, the better the rank the HEI gets. This phenomenon is inimical to quality education (Maharatna, 2014).

The market for higher education cannot do justice to those with merit and to those from the margins as money gains power to dominate the proceedings. The private HEIs give preferential treatment to under-represented students only on the basis of one's ability to pay and have been confined to only professional streams, bypassing the majority of students (Kapur and Mehta, 2007; Tilak, 2012; Nayak, 2014). Also the concept of technical efficiency is hardly tenable in the case of education as the educational production function does not exist in the strict sense (Majumdar 1983; Chattopadhyay 2010).

The market for higher education is characterized by selection-based efficiency and not exchange-based efficiency (Glennerster, 1991). The competition in a market requires that there should be a level playing field for the private and domestic institutions. However, most of the domestic institutions are not as well off as the foreign institutes are in terms of availability of resources. It would lead to competition between unequals, where the domestic HEIs are bound to lose. An attempt to introduce the market login will fail here because the price in an HEI is determined not by competition but by the amount of financial aid and donation they get. The market therefore, remains fragmented and hierarchical[16] (Winston, 1999; Chattopadhyay, 2010). Thus those HEIs in the lower ranks would fail to improve their quality.

7. Conclusion

The transition is taking place at a time when India is not really ready for two reasons. One, disparities in terms of caste, gender and region continue to be of relevance and two, quality-wise, India is far behind the international level even if we ignore the absence of the Indian HEIs in the world ranking. The growth of the private sector has been unregulated and other than a couple of good private universities, the remaining are engaged in commercial exploitation of the growing demand for higher education which is detrimental to the inclusive expansion and quality education as the private institutions resort to the subversion of the educational processes. The public universities continue to remain plagued by poor governance which is just an evasive word for corruption that is detrimental to the imparting of quality education and research. All these have led to poor degrees of employability of the graduates.

The very effort to achieve efficiency in the higher education system is contradictory to the aforesaid objectives of excellence, equity and expansion particularly in a developing country like India. Any effort to take recourse to cost minimization would lead to deterioration in the quality (excellence) of higher education because there exists a positive relationship between quality and cost. The series of reform measures mooted and implemented have sought to construct a regulated market for higher education with consumers being given more and more sovereignty while the private providers have expressed unhappiness over the excessive regulations they have been subjected to. At the same time, there has been a move towards giving more autonomy to the HEIs. Among many other moves to encourage the private sector, there is an unmistakable emphasis on fostering public-private partnerships (PPP) to rope in the private sector. Even through the state level Higher Education Councils, the private initiatives are now eligible for government aid.

Notes

1. Revenue augmentation measures included encouraging tax compliance, hike in user charges to mobilize more non-tax revenue and disinvestment of public assets.
2. SAP and the stabilization package together constitute the Washington Consensus as both the institutions are located at the Washington D.C. Neoliberalism as an ideology, arguably, informs Washington Consensus.

3. The Supreme Court in its landmark judgment allowed the private investors in higher education to make reasonable surplus and use it for the purpose of reinvestment rather than not to make profit by commercialization of the enterprise.
4. Choice making by students has to be based on information to make it meaningful as choices made are irreversible in the context of education and education being an 'experience good', furnishing of information can never be adequate.
5. Higher education can be considered to be a quasi-public item of goods which is assumed to have both the 'privateness' and 'publicness'. It is for public good because the externalities are generated but at the same time it is exclusive.
6. Negotiated mode of funding involves allocation on the basis of the previous year and providing incremental funds on the broadly laid formula.
7. It involves importing of ideas, techniques and practices from the private sector in order to make the public sector more business-like.
8. Retrieved from Reference Note, Lok Sabha Sceretariat, No. 21/RN/Ref./2014.
9. Central Universities and State Universities combined.
10. Annual Reports, UGC, Various Years.
11. https://mygov.in/new-education-policy-group.html.
12. http://www.ugc.ac.in/pdfnews/8023719_Guidelines-for-CBCS.pdf.
13. It entails opening up of public education services to private sector participation on a for-profit basis and using the private sector to design, manage or deliver aspects of public education
14. Even the economists who subscribe to the market principles have viewed education and its financing differently. Becker (1975) has shown why public funding is necessary to give the best of the opportunities to the meritorious. Funding of education illustrates the case where there exists no trade-off between efficiency and equity. For efficiency, equalization of opportunities to education is a pre-requisite.
15. Ideally, the objective of an HEI is prestige maximization in the absence of profit maximization.
16. Those HEIs at the top would attract the best of the minds and resources whereas those at the lower positions would not.

References

Abrol, D. 2010. Governance of Indian Higher Education: An Alternate Proposal. *Social Scientist.* Vol. 38/Nos. 9–12 September-December 2010.

Ball, Stephen and Deborah Youdell. 2007. Hidden Privatization in Public Education. *Education International*. University of London: Institute of Education.

Becker, Gary. 1975. *Human Capital: A Theoretical and Empirical Analysis, with Special Reference to Education*. New York: Columbia University Press.

Carnoy, Martin. 1995. Structural Adjustment and the changing face of education. *International Labour Review*. Vol. 134, No. 6. pp. 653–673.

Chattopadhyay, S. 2009. The market in higher education. Concern for equity and quality. *Economic and Political Weekly*. July 18.

Chattopadhyay, S. 2010. An Elitist and flawed approach towards higher education. *Economic and Political Weekly*. May 1.

Chattopadhyay, S, *Education and Economics*, Oxford University Press, New Delhi, 2012.

Das, Dipendra Nath and Chattopadhyay, S. 2014. Academic performance indicators. *Economic and Political Weekly*. December 13.

Duraisamy, P. and M. Duraisamy. 2015. *On the Privatization, Economic Burden of Expenditure on Households, and Role of Student Loan in Financing Higher Education in India*. Paper presented at an international seminar on Innovative Methods of Financing of Higher Education during February 23–25, 2015 at NUEPA. New Delhi (Draft).

Glennerster, H. 1991. Quasi-market for Education? *The Economic Journal*. Vol. 101, No. 408. September, pp. 1268–1276.

Government of India. 1997. *Government Subsidies in India. Discussion Paper*. Ministry of Finance, Department of Economic Affairs, New Delhi, May.

Government of India. 2000. *Report on a Policy Framework for Reforms in Education*. New Delhi, April.

Government of India. 2005. *Report of the Central Advisory Board of Education (CABE) Committee on Autonomy of Higher Education*. New Delhi: Ministry of Human Resource Development.

Government of India. 2008. *Eleventh Five Year Plan (2007–12). Social Sector*. Vol. 2. Planning Commission of India, New Delhi: OUP.

Government of India. 2009. *National Knowledge Commission. Report to the Nation 2006–09*. National Knowledge Commission, Delhi.

Government of India. 2009. *Report of the Committee to Advise on Renovation and Rejuvenation of Higher Education*. UGC, Delhi.

Government of India. 2010. *UGC Regulations on Minimum Qualifications for Appointment of Teachers and Other Academic Staff in Universities and Colleges and Measures for Maintenance of Standards in Higher Education*. The Gazette of India, September 18, Delhi.

Government of India. 2012. *Committee on Report of Participation in Higher Education: Report of NR Narayana Murthy Committee*, New Delhi.

Government of India. 2013. *Rashtriya Uchattar Shiksha Abhiyan*. Ministry of Human Resource Development.

Government of India. 2013. *Twelfth Five Year Plan (2012–17). Social Sectors.* Vol. 3. Planning Commission of India. New Delhi: Sage Publication.

Government of India. 2013. *UGC Regulations for Mandatory Accreditation*. The Gazette of India, January, Delhi.

Government of India. 2014. *All India Survey of Higher Education*. Ministry of Human Resource Development, New Delhi.

Gurukkal, Rajan. 2015. Scrapping the UGC. Corporate Agenda Under Knowledge Economy. *Economic and Political Weekly*, May 2.

https://mygov.in/new-education-policy-group.html.

http://www.ugc.ac.in/pdfnews/8023719_Guidelines-for-CBCS.pdf.

Jongbloed, B.. 2004. Regulation and Competition In Higher Education, in Pedro Texeira, Ben Jongbloed, David Dill and Alberto Amaral (eds). *Markets in Higher Education: Rhetoric or Reality?* London/Boston/Dordrecht: Kluwer Publishers.

Kapur, Devesh and Pratap Bhanu Mehta. 2007. *Indian Higher Education Reform: From Half-baked Socialism to Half-baked Capitalism*. Prepared for Presentation at the Brookings-NCAER India Policy Forum 2007. New Delhi.

Lok Sabha Secretariat. 2014. *Budget for Education Sector in India.* Reference Note No. 21/RN/ReF./2014. Maharatna, Arup. 2014. Invasion of Educational Universe by Neo-liberal Economic thinking: A Civilization Casualty?. *Economic and Political Weekly,* September 13.

Majumdar, Tapas. 1983. *Investment in Education and Social Choice*. New York: Cambridge University Press.

Nayak, Dhanwanti. 2014. Understanding the Logic of Neo-liberalism in Education. *Economic and Political Weekly*, March 29.

Sharma, V. 2010. UPA's Agenda of Academic 'Reforms' Facilitating Trade in Higher Education. *Social Scientist*, Vol. 38/Nos. 9–12, September-December 2010.

Tilak, J.B.G. 2004. Public Subsidies in Education in India. *Economic and Political Weekly*, January 24.

Tilak, J.B.G. 2010. Policy Crisis in Higher Education: Reform or Deform?. *Social Scientist*. Vol. 38/Nos. 9–12 September-December 2010.

Tilak, J.B.G. 2012. Higher Education Policy in India in transition. *Economic and Political Weekly*, March 31.

Tilak, J.B.G. 2014. Private Higher Education in India. *Economic and Political Weekly*, October 4. UGC. Annual Reports. Various years.

Winston, G.C. 1999. Subsidies, Hierarchy and Peers: The Awkward Economics of Higher Education. *The Journal of Economic Association*, Vol. 13, No. 1, Winter. pp. 13–36.

3

Higher Education in India and China: Game Changer or Opportunity Lost?

G. Balatchandirane

A nation is advanced in proportion as education and intelligence spread among the masses. The chief cause of India's ruin has been the monopolizing of the whole education and intelligence of the land among a handful of men. If we are to rise again, we shall have to do it by spreading education among the masses.

—Swami Vivekananda, 1897

(Advaita Ashrama, 1987, p. 444)

At present, of all the countries in the world, India and China are best poised to reap the benefits that can come through the demographic dividend. The current wave of globalization and the knowledge economy—whose share is rising in both the countries—suggest that the benefits would be immense provided both the countries exploit the opportunities thrown up by their domestic demographic transitions and the recent trends in the international economy. The role of higher education is pivotal in this scheme of things as it provides the requisite human capital which is a *sine qua non* for the capturing of the benefits of the demographic dividend—in essence a rapid and sustained raising of the economic growth rates and income levels. In what follows we look at the performance of the higher education sector in both the countries in the recent past and what needs to be done keeping in mind the globalization trends and the rise of the knowledge economy.

For long, policy planners in the developing countries attached much less importance to higher education, compared to how they rated primary education. The reasons are not far to seek. In the post World War II years, as a large number of countries gained independence and tried to rapidly catch up with the advanced nations, they had to have their priorities clear. There was a huge shortage of resources and what was available had to be optimally utilized. While a number of these countries had untapped natural resources, they did not have the technology to exploit them. Industrial growth was hardly existent. The human resources too were underdeveloped as the colonial masters had never given any priority to the development of industry or the human capital of the countries they ruled. It was around this time that the seminal role of education was highlighted through the works of Theodore Schultz, Gary S. Becker and others. What was brought to the fore was the fact that the spending on educating the masses was not to be treated as expenditure, but as investment. Just as one could talk of physical capital accumulation as being necessary for industrial development, as investments in physical capital had their returns, these economists held that education played a similar role. Spending on educating the masses was an investment as it gave measurable economic returns to the individual and the society. The term 'human capital' entered the popular lexicon.

The rates of return studies which followed found that primary education had the highest returns, followed by secondary and then higher education which had the least rate of return in comparative terms. Second, for the same amount of investment, the rates of return were higher for developing countries as compared to developed countries. Third, the social rates of return were larger compared to the private rates of return. As the mass of the population in the developing world was illiterate, the policy prescription was to allocate large shares to the primary education sector and the government's energies were focused there. This approach ties well with the economic histories of countries in East Asia (Balatchandirane, 2014; Balatchandirane et al., 2001). While this focus on primary education made eminent economic sense, higher education was never accorded the importance it deserved. The Jomtien Conference in the early 1990s tended to reinforce the idea that primary education was the more important one.

Two more factors are held to be responsible for the decline in the importance attached to higher education in the decade of the 1980s. The first one has to do with the fact that in the developing world, the universities did not live up to the expectations placed on them; so disillusionment with them set in. Second, a number of them did not connect with issues that had relevance with their localities, or countries. The disconnect between the realities around these universities and the contents of what the universities taught was glaring and sometimes even worsened the existing social inequalities. Cumulatively, these factors led to the degradation of higher education institutions in the 1980s. Later, higher education seems to have gained the lost ground. The UN also has been producing a number of studies that imply the diverse contributions of higher education apart from the purely economic (Thomson, 2008). By the end of the 1980s, the higher education systems of China and India were woefully inadequate to cater to the needs of their huge populations.

Developments in the 1990s, however, tended to change the outlook on higher education. The first was the strengthening of the globalization trends which raised the demands for human capital as huge export opportunities opened up. The second was the rise in the knowledge economy. The requisite human capital could be created only by higher education institutions. Thus the higher education sector came to be looked upon with favour. However, for a variety of reasons governments were withdrawing from the social sector commitments; they encouraged the role of the private sector in higher education. As higher education is associated with very large externalities, public investments in it can be justified. But the neoliberal approaches of the day only encouraged this kind of promotion of higher education through the private sector.

How important is higher education to the economies of China and India? Higher education is held to be a "... specialized form of human capital, contribution of which to economic growth is very significant." Higher education helps in the rapid industrialization of the economy as it supplies manpower which is endowed with professional, technical and managerial skills. However, when we discuss about knowledge economies, its role is even more important as it supplies not just workers but knowledge workers. Finally, higher education facilitates the creation, absorption and dissemination of knowledge which is critical to rapid economic growth. It also facilitates globalization. A whole range of benefits flows when a substantial share of the population of country is educated at the higher education level. When we consider the Gross Enrolment Rate (GER) and the level of economic development, there is a strong correlation between the two. Without significant levels of enrolments in higher education, no nation in the world has become advanced. While high levels GERs do not automatically guarantee that a nation would become advanced, it is difficult to spot any country that is advanced but has a low level of GER in higher education. In other words, while a high level of GER in higher education is not a sufficient condition for a country to achieve the developed nation status, it is a necessary condition. The critical minimum threshold level seems to be 30 per cent GER in higher education (Tilak, 2003b; 2005). While the Indian GER for higher education is just over 20 per cent, China's is around 30 per cent.

In today's world, the rapid pace of technology advancement means that no country can afford to neglect its technology creation and absorption capabilities if it wants to develop. It would require a technological laggard a vast amount of time and effort to catch up with the developed world. It is the higher education sector that contributes to the building up of research and development capabilities in a country. There is a strong correlation between higher education and the level of technology in a country. It has been held that " ... the level of achievement in technology may be a close indicator of economic growth itself." Countries with high enrolments in higher education are leaders in technology, while those with poor achievements in technology invariably have low higher education enrolment rates (Tilak, 2003a). There are also very important strategic implications that flow from the possession of a large base of human capital (Balatchandirane, 2010).

What is the role and contribution of research universities? They are characterized by top graduates, cutting-edge research, and vigorous technology transfer. Their critical dimensions are a concentration of talent, abundance of resources and favourable governance, which combine to assure excellence in graduate education and research output. Nurturing research universities is the single strongest component of knowledge based systems, due to their crucial social, economic and cultural impact (Meek, 2009). Human capital, it is believed, has played a much more important role than so far suggested in the literature. The reduction in the total factor productivity declines in the recent past is attributed to the fact that there was a spurt in college enrolment in China in the decade from 1997 and there has been inefficient utilization of human capital. The larger point is that the role of human capital to economic growth is validated (Whalley et al., 2010).

Higher Education in China and India

Both China and India have expanded their higher education systems very rapidly in the last twenty-five years, although starting from a low base. In the late 1980s, India's GER in higher education was higher at 5 per cent to China's 3 per cent. But the situation has dramatically changed in recent years with China rapidly raising its GER and overtaking the Indian GER. The interesting feature is that when higher education expanded in the US and Europe in the 1960s and 1970s, they had high levels of GNP per capita but both China and India have shown rapid rises in enrolment rates in higher education of late with low levels of GNP per capita. While the expansion of higher education for the US and Europe had been at public expense, the current expansion of higher education in China and India is privately financed. China and India would be occupying the top two positions in terms of enrolments in higher education in the world in the near future. While China would have 37 million registered for higher education by 2020, the figure for India would be 28 million.

A large share of the increased demand for higher education is met by low-cost and low-quality mass institutions. A small share is met by high-quality elite institutions which are mainly public. While the mass institutions in China are in the state sector, they are in the private sector in India. Both the Governments seem to be focusing on a small number of elite institutions. Thus, in spite of the tremendous expansion of higher education systems in these two countries, the existing inequalities in access to higher education will not decline much. This is due to the fact that the higher education systems that are currently developing in both China and India are highly differentiated. Further, the public sector is increasingly displaced by the private sector in both the countries. Thus access to expensive private sector supplied higher education may not be affordable to the masses in China and India.

While inequities in higher education are high in both the countries, China seems to be worse off than India. Chinese higher education system is one of the most stratified and hierarchical in the world. Affirmative action aimed at increasing the access to education for various disadvantaged communities has been taking place in India for some time now. However, on issues of quickly expanding higher education and improving its quality, India is doing quite badly. As demand for higher education is high in both the countries, the Governments have shifted the costs to the families and reduced the public spending on it. While China depends on cost-sharing and user charges in higher education, India has been depending on the private sector for expansion. While China's public spending on higher education is a low of 0.5 per cent of GDP, it is even lesser in India. As much as three-fourths of Indian students in professional fields in higher education are studying at private institutions.

Barring a few elite institutions in both the countries which are good, the overall quality of higher education is quite low. China lays more emphasis on quality than India. Faculty shortage is an issue in both countries, with India having a serious shortage. Indian professors are better paid than their Chinese counterparts. With economic returns to investments in engineering education high, one finds that one-fourth of students in higher education in India and one-third in China are in engineering courses. The transition from postgraduate courses to PhD is 27 per cent in China, whereas it is just 1 per cent in India. In terms of planning, China has a clear long-term policy and is attempting through heavy investment in R&D in some elite institutions to raise the quality of education as well as the quantum of technological applications. India on the other hand has not displayed a clear policy of developing higher education and the State has been weak in controlling the forces of privatization that have been holding sway. India also faces major issues in terms of quality, equity and governance in higher education (Tilak, 2013a).

Higher Education in India

Growth

There was an impressive quantitative growth in higher education in both general and technical or professional fields in India after Independence as the base was small. The immediate needs for manpower could be met. The tremendous expansion seen in the two and a half decades following Independence as the existing base of higher education was small and there was a huge demand for it in Independent India. Second, modernizing India created demands for a huge and varied skilled personnel and higher education had to expand accordingly. Lastly, as a way to reduce existing inequalities in society, the State promoted equality of opportunity in higher education as well as public subsidies. From the mid-1970s while the number of higher education institutions increased at a slower rate, public expenditure on higher education fell rapidly leading to quality issues. By early 1990s, with the introduction of economic reforms, higher education was viewed much differently and cost recovery measures were increasingly introduced and the role of private finances in higher education was encouraged. In various ways, the notion of higher education as a public good got diluted and increasingly it was viewed as a private good.

Financing and Privatization

Around the mid-1980s, the World Bank's emphasis on elementary education as a way out of poverty for countries like India tended to lead to the conclusion that a cap should be placed on the growth of higher education. The consequence was the State's negligence towards higher education. Private sector's role in higher education expanded rapidly. Post 2000, with the increasingly greater realization of the need to build a knowledge economy, the State has gone into an overdive for massive expansion in higher education. However this was not publicly funded but depended on private as well as variations of the public-private participation models. (Tilak, 2013b) While it has been felt for a long time that public spending on education in India should be at least 6 per cent of GNP overall with 1.5 per cent going in for higher education, the actual spending since Independence has hardly ever crossed 4 per cent. This inadequacy of public funding is a major ailment of higher education in India. The public spending on higher education is just 0.5 per cent of GNP. Private spending on higher education because of large scale privatization could be about 2 per cent of GNP (Forbes, 2014).

The Indian State has in a large measure abdicated its responsibility towards the provision of education and this is in stark contrast to the role played by the East Asian countries like Japan. The rapid spread of private interests in higher education with which the State meekly acquiesced, has few parallels. Private interests, in the face of the failure of the State to provide education as enshrined in the Constitution, have exploited the system for their profit motives. Knowledge, a social asset, has increasingly been sought to be placed in the domain of private property. The wholesale privatization of education has resulted in the lowering of standards, the increasing of various social inequalities and the enhancement of opportunities for the dominant sections of society, thereby perpetuating the elitist social base. What stands out in the case of countries like Japan is the State's thorough planning and implementation, but above all, the commitment to the cause of education. The Indian State on the other hand has in addition to abdicating of its essential role steadily diluted its obligation (Balatchandirane, 2000).

Quality

One of the reasons for the falling quality of higher education in India is the fact that the rapid expansion in the last three decades has not been even across the board but confined to certain specific areas like engineering, pharmaceuticals, business, and computer applications. The number of engineering colleges as well as the enrolments in them has been rising at 20 per cent per annum for the last three decades. During the peak period of 1995–2010, on an average, one new engineering college and one management institute opened every day. In the span of the three decades between 1983 and 2013, students' admission to engineering colleges rose from 40,000 to 1.2 million or about 30–fold. The approved seats for admission were even higher at 1.5 million. During the same period, the total number of those completing PhDs in science and engineering just doubled and those attaining Master's degree in science and engineering only tripled. The availability of faculty members to keep up with even the quality 1983 levels of has been woefully short directly impacting the quality of higher education. Even at the very top, in the fifteen Indian Institutes of Technology, fully a third of the faculty positions—about 2000 openings—are yet to be filled up due to shortage of qualified persons.

The second issue is that 90 per cent of the public research spending in India is within the autonomous institutions, outside of the university system. The quality of graduate teaching is enhanced when the teacher is involved in research; likewise research benefits when the researcher is involved in teaching, which is seen in many world class universities in the world. The benefits of research are going to positively impact the innovation system. In East Asia, innovation that has flown from industrial development resulted in industrial in-house R&D and then ultimately in public scientific research. While competing in world markets, the strength of the innovation system in the country is enhanced when the industrial in-house R&D on one hand, and the investments in public scientific research of value to industry on the other, are healthy and benefit from each other. When research is combined with teaching, trained researchers emerge and can be valuable faculty staff. Thus future public investments in R&D need to be inside the university system. (Forbes, 2014)

Equitable Access

GER for higher education in India today is 19.4 per cent for the eligible cohorts (age 18–23). For males it is 20.8 and for females it is 17.9 per cent. However, there can be huge regional variations as seen in the figure of 8.1 for the State of Jharkhand and 35.9 for the State of Manipur. (MHRD, 2015) In addition to the inequities in terms of gender (which has been falling) and states, there are also other inequities in terms of rural/urban areas and rich/poor dichotomies. If one were to look at the geographical spread of engineering institutions in India, in the year 2013, five states (Tamil Nadu, Andhra Pradesh, Kerala, Karnataka and Maharashtra) accounting for 30 per cent of the total population admitted 60 per cent of all engineering students. Five more states (Madhya Pradesh, Gujarat, Orissa, Haryana and Punjab) accounting for 19 per cent of the population admitted 22 per cent of all engineering students. The rest of India accounting for 51 per cent of the population admitted just 18 per cent of all engineering students. A decade earlier, these figures were even more skewed (Forbes, 2014).

Chinese Universities and the National Innovation System

The national innovation system in China was formed in the 1950s, built on the Soviet model. The government played a preponderant role and the management and planning was heavily centralized. Universities were primarily expected to train people in Science and Technology. University based research activity was weak. This changed from 1978 when a number of public research institutes were set up. In 1979, these were explicitly recognized as centres for both teaching and research. This step was to tie the universities with the national innovation system. Now it was not just government affiliated research institutes alone but universities and the industrial sector too that became important players.

This paved the way for the universities to become an important force in the knowledge production. In 2004, about 437,000 full-time equivalent researchers were working in universities, accounting for 12.5 per cent of national R&D expenditures and publishing close to two-thirds of the research papers. Around this time, two-fifths of the basic research and over a quarter of the applied research was done by the universities. Funding has been coming from three sources. Firstly, three-fourths of total funding in 1985 was accounted for by the Government. This share came down but since 2000 has gone up to remain around half of the total funding the universities get for research. The second source of funding is from the industrial sector. Since 1985, funds from the industrial sector have risen steeply accounting today for about a third of total funding. The third source of funding is from the technology market where universities sell their patents and other intellectual products (Xue, 2006).

Applied research has been the more important aspect of R&D in the Chinese universities. In terms of research output, universities and colleges in China are a 'vital component' of the national innovation system. While the link between the universities and the government research institutes is weak that between the universities and industry has been very strong since 1978. In the Chinese context, these two entities have not been competing but complementing each other. Around 1978, there was a serious shortage of researchers in industry. On the other hand, universities had the human capital but were short of funds. This was to lead to strong links with universities supplying researchers as well as new knowledge. Further there are informal consulting by university researchers to industry, technology development contracts, technology transfer and licensing, joint research centres, and university-based science parks in major cities with strong entrepreneurial activities. Joint research centres are preferred by the industry as there is high quality human talent and strong foundations for research are readily available in the universities. The first of the university-based science parks was established in 1989 and today they represent a new avenue for commercializing technologies developed at the university. These science parks have been an important incubator for university-owned spin-offs. In 2004, of the about 4,500 enterprises affiliated to universities, about a fourth were located in science parks.

University-owned enterprises, unique to China are enterprises that are in one way or other controlled by the universities with which they are attached. They have been in existence since 1950s and they enable students to have short term internships or apprenticeships in an actual production environment. Initially, a number of university-owned enterprises were poorly managed and looked for short-term profits. The question of should universities run enterprises was raised in the 1980s. In the 1990s, China's State Council came out in support of such enterprises and actively encouraged them to develop higher education. This was a period of rapid growth for these enterprises. From 2000 onwards, once again controversies surfaced. Financial risks for the concerned universities were an issue. As they became more commercialized, some of them broke their links with the universities to become separate entities. These enterprises are publicly traded on the stock market. These listed companies have been useful in converting new technologies into applications and secondly in addressing the financial requirements of the university.

Towards the end of the 1980s, R&D activities were divorced from the production processes and the market. This was when the Chinese Government passed the resolution on the Structural Reform of the Science and Technology System in China. The basic idea was to make China's research organization directly serve the needs of national economic development. Changes were to be made in the funding system, technology markets were to be established and new approaches were to be made to the management of the research organization, etc. The idea was to make the R&D organization responsive to market needs. The Government appropriation came down as a source of income for Public Research Institutes. Funding for universities came down to half of what they got earlier. Universities tended to diversity their sources of funding by turning to industry as the major source of income. Industry funding accounted for about half of total research income and ties with industry became strong. On the negative side, the pursuit of finance and hence industry funding have led to commercialization of university functioning which may not be good in the long run. Too much commercial activity on campus has in some places led to the neglect of basic research. Being too close to the market can have a negative bearing on the functioning of these universities (Xue, 2006).

Globalization Opportunities

A simple definition of globalization holds it to be "... the accelerated movement of goods, services, capital, people and ideas across national borders". The phenomenon of globalization is nothing new, but there are some qualitative differences compared to the earlier phases. The collapse of the Breton Woods system and the liberalization of trade and finance coupled with the improvements in the speed and costs of communications have impacted the current phase of globalization, which "is marked out by the sheer rapidity of change and by the ever-growing power of multinational corporations". (Little and Green, 2009) As this coalesces with the onset of the knowledge economy and the rise in the demand for knowledge workers, the need for human capital trained in higher educational institutions has been booming. Countries like China and India, with their large demographic advantage have much to gain.

One major point to note is that with the increasing integration of markets across borders, the movement of goods, services, capital, labour as well as technology across countries is facilitated tremendously. Be it for the production of increasingly sophisticated goods and services that are in demand, or the need for highly qualified human capital, or the creation of new ideas or technology, the expectations placed on the university systems in China and India are very large. How they cope with this in quantitative and qualitative terms is going to have a major impact on how the opportunities are going to be exploited and how this will impact on the economic growth of these two countries.

Globalization, it has been pointed out, has impacted the nation-states in a way that they have steadily withdrawn from higher education as seen particularly in the reduction of public resources. The competition for resources pits the universities between the State and the market. This has led to a significant reduction in the autonomy thus far enjoyed by both the universities and their professionals both from the nation-states and markets (Ordorika, 2009). Globalization has led to the stepping back of the State from direct control of higher education to a state supervisory model. There is a movement towards the market steering of higher education expecting an enhancement of efficiency and accountability, while at the same time reducing the financial burden of higher education on the state.

The Demographic Dividend

Of late, the infant and child mortality rates in a number of developing countries, including India and China, have fallen. While on the one hand, this has led to an appreciable fall in the total fertility rates, simultaneously this has resulted in a baby boom in the short run. This ultimately translates into a higher share of working age population. The second important point to note is that the existence of the large share of young population will not exist indefinitely. In a few decades' time both India and China will lose this potential advantage, with the window of opportunity closing in China earlier than in India. This advantage is called the demographic dividend. Basically it refers to the few decades when population of a country undergoes a significant transition. The rapid falls in child and infant mortality rates leads to a fall in fertility rates and ultimately to a significant rise in the share of the youth in population. This means the dependency ratios will be healthy. In other words, there will be the availability of human and other resources which can ensure a high rate of economic growth.

Table 1: Age structure of the Indian and Chinese Populations in 2015

Age Group (yrs) / *Country*	*0–14 years*	*15–24*	*25–54*	*55–64*	*65 and above*
India	28.09	18.06	40.74	7.16	5.95
China	17.08	13.82	47.95	11.14	10.01

Source: CIA, 2015.

Currently, India and China are two countries with the largest numbers of youth population in the world. The noteworthy points are (a) the sheer absolute number of youth population, (b) the recent rapid rise in their numbers, and (c) how long will these demographic dividends last? As shown in Table 1, close to 46 per cent of Indian population and about 31 per cent of the Chinese population are below the age of 25. The potential demographic dividend that can accrue to the economy is immense. When we consider the economically productive age group of 15–64 years which is usually defined as the 'working age' population, 66 per cent of the Indian population and 73 per cent of the Chinese population fall in this category. The median age of Indian population was 27 years and that of the Chinese population was 37 years in 2015.

In concrete terms, how can a country exploit the demographic dividend? Three mechanisms related to labour supply, savings, and human capital have been pointed out. With respect to labour supply, the children born during the phase when fertility rates were high (the 'baby boomers') would on reaching adulthood enter the labour force in large numbers. Importantly the labour market should be able to absorb them and they should have been adequately educated and trained. Second, the falling fertility rates indicate that with a smaller family size, women enter the workforce in larger numbers. They are likely to be more educated than the older cohorts. Both of these would impact productivity positively. The critical assumption here is that the government proactively creates an enabling environment in terms of creation of jobs, setting up of educational and training institutions and related measures.

When we look at the second mechanism of savings, three factors need to be noted. Firstly, as there is a rise the number of those of working age, the total savings get enlarged as the working age population typically tends to earn more and save more compared to the dependent population. With increased savings, there can be higher investment and hence growth in the country. Second, as the people move to the 40 to 65 age bracket, the investment in children declines (who have become income earners themselves) and savings for retirement increase. Third, the private household savings translate into capital that helps finance growth. East Asia is a typical example.

In the third mechanism of human capital, some relevant issues need to be looked at. As the family size reduces through demographic transition, investments in human capital rise. While this might be the least visible, it is the most significant. As mortality rates fall, the life expectancies rise; this impacts how the society views education, retirement, women's role and work. People are now more valuable assets. Second, as those with higher levels of education tend to have higher income levels, and as life expectancies rise, parents tend to have lesser number of children but educate them more and more. The net effect of higher investment in education is that is that the returns raise the productivity of labour which ultimately leads to higher wages and hence higher standards of living. In other words, economic growth as well as economic development tends to take place (Bloom et al., 2003).

The important caveat for the above mechanisms to function so that there is a spurt in economic growth is that there should be an enabling environment. Labour market should be able to expand and absorb new entrants. There should be efficient channelizing of investment to productive areas. Provisioning of high quality education and health care is a basic prerequisite. The important aspects about the demographic dividend is that it is time constrained, i.e., it lasts only for a limited period of time. And its flow is not automatic. Namely, there should be specific policies in place to maximally utilize the resources that would be released due to the falling birth rates which alter the age distribution of a population. (Bloom et al., 2003, Ross 2004) Stated differently, the various proactive roles of the government in ensuring that an enabling environment is provided is critical. The East Asian economic miracle was made possible as these countries created institutions and policies that enabled them to exploit the growth potential that was unleashed by the demographic transition these countries underwent. (Bloom et al., 1997).

In the light of the above, it is worth looking at the Indian context where there seems to be a presumption that there will be automatic benefits from the existence of the high share of young population. The specific inputs that need to be made on the education and health fronts seem to be lost sight of. Only when the youth section of the population is invested with high levels of human capital, in addition to being gainfully employed, can it help the country tap the vast opportunities for exporting various goods and services. Without the right policies being put in place, a country like India could find that the demographic dividend can lead to a demographic disaster—namely, a situation where it is saddled with a large working-age population that is unemployed or under employed. This is bound to have very serious consequences for the stability of the country (Chandrashekar et al., 2006; Bloom, 2011).

The demographic transition in India is believed to have started about 1970 and is expected to last till about 2030 or so. As much as one-fourth of the expected increase in the world population aged 15–64 between 2010 and 2040 will take place in India. And the demographic dividend so far has been large. 40 to 50 per cent of the per capita income growth is attributable to the current demographic dividend. Further it has been established that the causation flows from the demographic variables to income growth. And it holds out more advantages. About 69 per cent of the Indian population will be in this age bracket in 2040 making India the largest contributor to the global workforce till 2040. This also gives an opportunity for India to 'catch up' with China (Aiyar et al., 2011). In India's population pyramid the "bulge", namely, the 15–64 age bracket is expected to rise from 761 million in 2011 to about 869 million in 2020 when it would be the world's youngest country with an average age of 29 years and also account for 28 per cent of the world's workforce. The average age would be 37 years for China and the US and 45 years in Western Europe. About two-thirds of India's population will be in the age bracket of 15–59 years by 2026. As China's demographic dividend starts falling from the peak from 2015, India will have the advantage till about 2035 or 2040 (Ernest and Young, 2013; Ladu Singh et al., 2011).

Based on an analysis of data over 1961–2003, it was found that GDP per capita growth was positively related to the growth differential between the working-age population and the total population. It was negatively related to child and old age dependency ratios. 46 per cent of economic growth in per capita GDP in China and 39 per cent in India during this period can be explained by the population dynamics. Till

2050, the population dynamics is expected to have a positive effect on India while impacting China negatively (Choudhry et al., 2010). Other studies (Aiyar et al., 2011) found similar trends, for instance, the growth acceleration in the 1980 has been found to be attributable to the country's changing age structure. The demographic dividend might add two percentage points per annum to the per capita GDP growth till about 2030 in the case of India.

The knowledge economy

Increasingly we talk about the movement of various countries in the direction of the knowledge economy; the sheer scale of the Chinese and Indian economies ensures that a sizeable part of them are increasingly identified as being in the realm of knowledge economies. The reasons are not far to seek. Both have large youth population, both have tremendous economic potential and both are well poised to meet the requirements of the knowledge economy if they address certain deficits in the economy and also ensure an enabling environment.

A knowledge economy is one where innovation is the more important activity compared to the exploitation of natural resources. In a knowledge economy, the economic activity shifts more and more towards the production, trading and consumption of knowledge. The absence of resources does not impede economic growth and now labour costs are no more a significant factor. Innovation is critical and is premised on the availability of two factors, namely, a substantial pool of human capital and a healthy rate of R&D spend.

The rise in the knowledge intensity of economic activities in reflected in what has come to be called as the knowledge economy. The knowledge—based economy has been defined as one where 'the production, diffusion and use of technology and information are key to economic activity and sustainable growth' (OECD, 1999, p. 7 cited in George, 2006). Investment in knowledge refers to investment in areas that generate knowledge, such as research and development, software, education and basic science. It also refers to 'innovation' and

Table 2: Forecast Gross Expenditures on R&D

		2012			*2013*			*2014*		
		GDP PPP BII, US$	*R&D as % GDP*	*GERD* PPP BII, US$*	*GDP PPP*	*R&D as % GDP BII, US$*	*GERD PPP*	*GDP PPP BII, US$*	*R&D as % GDP*	*GERD PPP BII, US$*
1	United States	15,940	2.8%	447	16,195	2.8%	450	16,616	2.8%	465
2	China	12,610	1.8%	232	13,568	1.9%	258	14,559	2.0%	284
3	Japan	4,704	3.4%	160	4,798	3.4%	163	4,856	3.4%	165
4	Germany	3,250	2.8%	92	3,266	2.8%	92	3,312	2.9%	92
5	South Korea	1,640	3.6%	59	1,686	3.6%	61	1,748	3.6%	63
6	France	2,291	2.3%	52	2,296	2.3%	52	2,319	2.3%	52
7	United Kingdom	2,375	1.8%	43	2,408	1.8%	44	2,454	1.8%	44
8	India	4,761	0.9%	40	4,942	0.85%	42	5,194	0.9%	44
9	Russia	2,555	1.5%	38	2,593	1.5%	38	2,671	1.5%	40
10	Brazil	2,394	1.3%	30	2,454	1.3%	31	2,515	1.3%	33
Subtotal (Top 40)		73,362	2.0%	1,478	75,338	2.0%	1,518	77,896	2.0%	1,576
Rest of World		10,071	0.4%	39	10,413	0.4%	40	10,837	0.4%	42
Global Spending		83.434	1.8%	1,517	85,751	1.8%	1,558	88,733	1.8%	1,618

Source: Battelle and R&D Magazine 2013.

the machinery, equipment and infrastructure to support it. What this essentially implies is that knowledge is the prime driver of economic growth and this highlights the primary role of human capital and technology in development (Varghese, 2013). It has also been pointed out that Tertiary Education Institutions support knowledge-driven economic growth strategies and poverty reduction by 1. Training a qualified and adaptable labour force, 2. Generating new knowledge, and 3. Building the capacity to access existing stores of global knowledge and to adapt that knowledge to local use (World Bank, 2002). Tertiary Education institutions are unique in their ability to integrate and create synergy among these three dimensions. The cornerstone of a knowledge society is higher education and advanced research.

R&D Spend

The Gross Domestic Expenditure on R&D (GERD) is given by the sum of R&D expenditures in the four sectors of business, university, government and non-profit institutions. The preceding Table 2 highlights the fact that India has been spending just about 0.9 per cent of its GDP on GERD while that of China is double of that. However as pointed out by Table 3, the gap between India and China in GERD spend is quite large and what is more, the gap has been increasing. While the share of the US in the total global spend has been slightly falling, that of China has been rising, while that of India has been constant. If the present trends continue, China's total funding of R&D is expected to overtake that of the US by 2022.

Further even when we see other parameters like the total number of researchers, the number of scientific papers published etc., China is ahead of India, by a good margin. The recent growth of knowledge-intensive industries should not lead one to think that India is well placed on the path to knowledge economy. There are both quantitative and qualitative issues that have to be reckoned with. The rapid industrial expansion partly due to the opportunities thrown up by increasing global integration has resulted in a large

Table 3: Share of Total Global R&D Spending

	2012	*2013*	*2014*
America (21)	**34.5%**	**34.0%**	**33.9%**
US	32.0%	31.4%	31.1%
Asia (20)	**37.0%**	**38.3%**	**39.1%**
China	15.3%	18.6%	17.6%
Japan	10.5%	10.5%	10.2%
India	2.7%	2.7%	2.7%
Europe (34)	**23.1%**	**22.4%**	**21.7%**
Germany	6.1%	5.9%	5.7%
Rest of the World (36)	**5.4%**	**5.3%**	**5.3%**

Source: Battelle and R&D Magazine 2013.

demand for skilled personnel as well as specific human capital which is in short supply. On the qualitative front, just a small share of the graduates is found by the MNCs to be of global standard. (Balatchandirane, 2012) While the total number of graduates passing out each year is almost double the number China produces, less than 5 per cent have the basic vocational skills. The figures for Korea is 96 per cent, for Germany 75 per cent and for the US 68 per cent. It is also held that just about 25 per cent of the engineers that India produces have the language skills, practical knowledge and cultural attitudes that enables them to work for MNCs (Battlle Corporation, 2010). China spent $ 213 trillion PPP in 2012 on total intramural expenditure on R&D. India spent $ 32 trillion PPP in 2011. China had 1020 researchers per million in 2012. India had 210 in 2010. In 2012 China surpassed the US as the largest recipient of patents (ESCAP, 2014).

The correlation between the amount spent on R&D by a country and the scientists and engineers per million population that it has is brought out in the Figure 1. The sizes of the balloons indicate the actual amount spent by each country on R&D. What comes out clearly is that the spend on R&D, and the creation of human capital, which is critical for the knowledge economy are strongly linked. One observes that most of the countries seem to be on the diagonal indicating that a rise in one leads to a rise in the other. Alternatively, countries that have low spending on R&D have low numbers of scientists and engineers per million population. One has to keep in mind the fact that while the current spend on R&D is indicated in the diagram, the human capital build-up has been influenced by the cumulative spending over the recent past.

With few exceptions, while the developing nations are clustered around the bottom left area, the developed nations with a history of higher levels of R&D spend occupy the centre and the top right area. The other noteworthy point is that despite China being on a level that is far lower compared to Japan, in absolute terms it spends the same

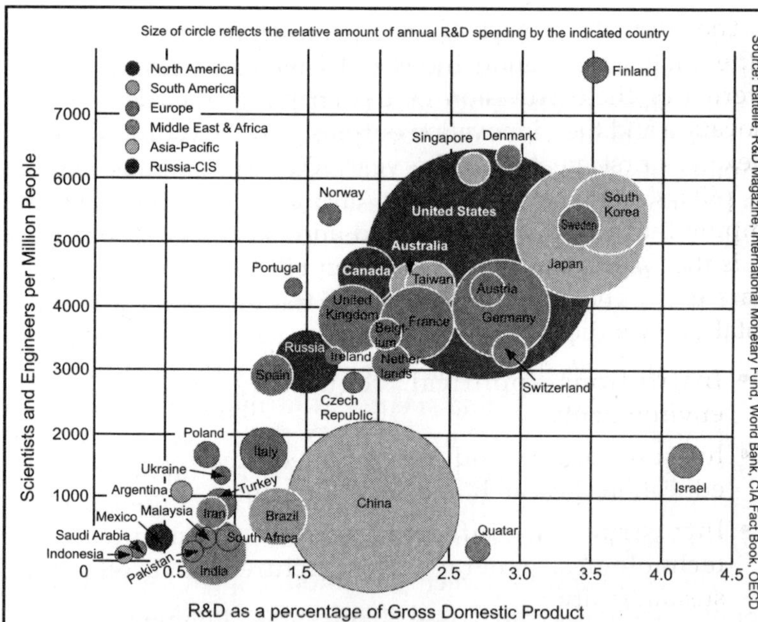

Figure 1: Link between R&D spend and human capital
Source: Battelle and R&D Magazine 2013.

amount as Japan does. India spends as much as the UK or France or South Korea again in absolute terms. While on a per capita basis both India and China spend much less than the advanced countries, India is way behind China. Why are these two countries behind others who spend almost the same absolute amount on R&D in terms of the human capital created? The answer is in the fact that the diagram is a snapshot view. It does not tell us the amounts spent on R&D historically. If we see the historical spending patterns, the cumulative spending on R&D by today's advanced nations is huge; that is key in explaining why their current numbers of scientists and engineers per million people is so high. From this flows one important lesson: no country can build valuable human capital overnight. Consistent high spending over the long term alone can guarantee this.

The ultimate impact of the spend of R&D is captured in the Global Innovation Index (GII) which ranks countries in terms of their provision of the enabling environment to innovation and their innovation outputs. The Global Innovation Index was first created in the year 2007 and over the years the 'pillars' and the 'sub pillars' and other metrics used to compute the GII have been refined and expanded. The latest one is the GII 2014 and this has seven pillars, with three sub-pillars each. The sub-pillars use 3 to 6 indicators leading to a total of 84 indicators. The pillars are:

- Institutions—political, regulatory and business environments.
- human capital and research—education, tertiary education, Research and Development.
- Infrastructure—information and communication technologies, general infrastructure and ecological sustainability.
- Market sophistication—credit, investment, and trade and competition.
- Business sophistication—knowledge workers, innovation linkages, and knowledge absorption.

- Knowledge and technology outputs—knowledge creation, knowledge impact, and knowledge diffusion.
- Creative outputs—intangible assets, creative goods and services, and online creativity.

Three of the seven pillars and a large number of the indicators have to do with education, human capital, knowledge economy and the like. GII 2014 found that without exception all the top 25 economies are in the high income group. China despite being an upper-middle income country which is edging close to the top 25, and at the current pace likely to reach the top 25 in a few years. India, on the other hand has been consistently falling in its ranks, with the greatest fall in the last one year period, when it slipped ten positions from 66 to 76. India's drastic fall in the ranks is attributed to the challenges it faces in integrating its efforts along the different dimensions of innovation to sustain a high level of innovation success.

Table 4: Global Innovation Index Rankings of India and China

Year	*Number of Countries covered*	*India*	*China*
2007	107	23	29
2008–2009	130	41	37
2009–2010	132	56	43
2011	125	62	29
2012	141	64	34
2013	142	66	35
2014	143	76	29

Source: Global Innovation Index, various years.

Other important points that emerge from GII 2014 are:

- The regions with the highest numbers of people with tertiary education and with the highest enrolment ratios in higher education are also those with the most researchers as a proportion of the total population.

- R&D is generally unprofitable in countries with low levels of human capital.
- China has not only been extensively expanding its higher education system, but has enlarged its research system even more.
- Graduates of tertiary arts programmes are among the most likely to contribute to product or service innovation.

Conclusions

Demographic changes in India now and China sometime back have led to a situation where there can be a demographic dividend—namely, the bulge in the working-age population with its attendant benefits—which can be exploited by both the countries (more so in the case of India). A number of opportunities at the international level due to globalization and rapidly expanding market opportunities can be exploited. The rise of the knowledge economy has thrown open even more windows of opportunity to both the countries. However, appropriate policies aimed at the provisioning of higher education to the burgeoning youth population is a must. Higher education also needs to be affordable. In terms of access, equity and quality, there are a number of issues that need to be tackled. Handled well, the demographic dividend is going to pay rich returns; mishandled, it could transfigure into a devastating demographic disaster.

Recent studies (for instance, Price Waterhouse Cooper, 2014) have been talking of how the Indian economy can grow at 9 per cent per annum for the next two decades and easily become a $10 trillion economy. The per capita income levels which are currently at $1500 would rise to about $ 7,000 during this period. This is possible only if a number of challenging areas are addressed. One of them is the field of education where seven million *additional* children would have to be imparted high quality formal education every year for the next twenty years. The investments in both human and physical capital as well as investments in R&D and innovation is a sine quo non. The experience of East Asia clearly holds lessons in this regard (Balatchandirane, 2005; 2007).

The increasing privatization of higher education also does not bode well. Creation of a few elite higher educational institutions which can be showpieces and the neglect of massification of higher education will lead to increases in existing social inequities. Addressing income inequalities in a society is one way to correct existing economic inequities. For this, endowing the population with near equal human capital is a must. While differences in individual capabilities is going to ensure that there will be differences in income levels, the State cannot exacerbate the economic inequalities by providing access to higher education in an inequitable way.

That brings us to the next point which relates to the role of the State. Suffused as we are with neoliberal approaches to most things, we tend to lose sight of certain essential roles of the State. One basic duty of the State is to ensure that the access, equity, quality and governance issues of higher education are evenly handled. An enabling environment has to exist before the dividends from the demographic transition can be realized. Failure to do so is going to lead to lost economic growth as well as a rise in social tensions.

Finally, a leaf out of the recent US response to the perceived decline in American Science and Technology might be instructive. The possibility that US may not remain number one in Science and Technology led to a lot of soul searching among academicians and policy makers. In 2005, a high power committee was set up to study the issue and give recommendations. The Report, published in 2007, was titled *Rising Above the Gathering Storm: Energizing and Employing America for a Brighter Economic Future*. The Report said that "... the committee is deeply concerned that the scientific and technological building blocks critical to our economic leadership are eroding at a time when many other nations are gathering strength." The recommended corrective actions related to four areas of which three focused on education, two of which dealt with higher education and research. The report also bemoaned the fact that higher education was suffering because of a fall in public funding and how it was critical to consider the 'public good' nature of higher education.

A follow up to the original Report was published by the same Committee in 2010 called *The Gathering Storm Report Revisited* in which they pointed out that the earlier trends had only strengthened in the five year period since then. The follow up Report urged even more efforts to make the US competitive by investing in education. The Gathering Storm Committee concluded in its original report that the only answer is through innovation. The clinching fact was that over the past half-century, 50 per cent to 85 per cent of the increase in the GDP of US is attributable to advancements in science and engineering. Thus faced with threats to its supremacy in science and technology, the US is discovering the merits of public funding for education and makes out a case for it domestically, while it has been telling the rest of the world about the merits of the market driven policies in higher education all along. It is high time India and China realize what is at stake. All the more so, given the great promise of the demographic dividend in the current situation of a rising share of knowledge economy in these two countries and the globalization trends.

References

2014 Global R&D Funding Forecast. *Battelle and R&D Magazine*, 2013.

Advaita Ashrama, *The Complete Works of Swami Vivekananda*, 7th edition, Vol. 5, Calcutta, 1987.

Aiyar, Shekhar and Ashoka Mody 2011. 'The Demographic Dividend: Evidence from the Indian States', International Monetary Fund, IMF Working Paper WP/11/38.

Bloom, David E. 2011. 'Population Dynamics in India and Implications for Economic Growth'. Harvard Institute for Global Health, PGDA Working Paper No. 65.

Bloom, David E., and Jeffrey G. Williamson 1997. 'Demographic Transitions and Economic Miracles in Emerging Asia', Cambridge: National Bureau of Economic Research Working Paper 6268.

Bloom, David E., David Canning and Jaypee Sevilla 2003. *The Demographic Dividend: A New Perspective on Economic Consequences of Population Change.* Rand: Santa Monica.

Central Intelligence Agency 2015. The World Fact Book https://www.cia.gov/library/publications/the-world-factbook/ Accessed on 15th September 2015.

Chandrashekar, C.P., Jayati Ghosh and Anamitra Roychowdhury 2006. "The 'Demographic Dividend' and Young India's Economic Future: *Economic and Political Weekly,* Vol. XLI, No. 49, (December 9): pp. 5055–5064.

Choudhry, Misbah T. and J. Paul Elhorst, 2010. 'Demographc transition and economic growth in China, India and Pakistan', *Economic Systems* 34: 218–236.

Ernst & Young and FICCI 2013. 'Reaping India's Promised Demographic Dividend—Industry in Driving Seat', 17 October.

Forbes, Naushad 2014. 'Higher Education in India: Growth with Challenges' in Cornell University et al., pp. 85–91.

George, Elizabeth St 2006. 'Positioning Higher Education for the Knowledge Based Economy' *Higher Education* 52 (4), 589–610.

Govindswamy, Balatchandirane 2000. "State and Education: India's Failures and Japanese Lessons", *Journal of the Japanese Association for South Asian Studies,* (Tokyo), No. 12, (October), pp. 175–202.

Govindswamy, Balatchandirane 2012. "Strategic Implications of human capital Today" in *Grand Strategy for India: 2020 and Beyond* eds. Krishnappa Venkatshamy and Princy George, pp. 146–161. New Delhi: Pentagon Security International.

Govindswamy, Balatchandirane 2005. "Human Capital in the Modernization of Japan and India", *The Indian Journal of Labour Economics,* Vol. 48, No. 3, (July-September), 605–18.

Govindswamy, Balatchandirane 2007. "India's BRICs Ambitions, human capital and Japanese Lessons" in *India and Japan in Search of Global Roles,* eds Rajaram Panda and Yoo Fukazawa, pp. 182–210. New Delhi: Promilla & Co., Publishers in association with Bibliophile South Asia and Japan Foundation.

Govindswamy, Balatchandirane 2014."Reconstruction and Development: Relevance of the Korean Experience in Education". In *AFFINITIES, India and Korea: Past and Present* eds. Pankaj Mittal, Daisy and Ravi Bhushan, pp. 172–184. New Delhi: D.K. Printworld (P) Ltd.

Govindswamy, Balatchandirane, Rajiv Ranjan and Sreemati Chakrabarti 2001. "Basic Education and Economic Development: A Comparative Study of Japan, China and India", *International Studies,* Vol. 38, No. 3, (July), pp. 229–75.

Ladusingh, Laishram and M.R. Narayana 2011. 'Demographic Dividends for India: Evidence and Implications Based on National Transfer Accounts', Asian Development Bank: ADB Economics Working Paper Series No. 292.

Little, Angela and W. Andy Green 2009. "Successful globalisation, education and sustainable development", *International Journal of Educational Development* Vol. 29, pp. 166–174.

Meek, V. Lynn, Ulrich Teichler, Mary-Louise Kearney (eds.) 2009. 'Higher Education, Research and Innovation: Changing Dynamics Report on the UNESCO Forum on Higher Education, Research and Knowledge 2001–2009', International Centre for Higher Education Research, Kassel.

MHRD 2015 *Gross enrolment ratio (GER) in Higher Education http://www.data. gov.in catalog/gross-enrolment-ratio-ger-higher-education#web_catalog_tabs_block_10* Accessed on 5th Feb. 2015.

Ordorika, Imanol 2009. "Commitment to society: contemporary challenges for public research universities" in Global University Network for Innovation (ed.) *Higher Education at a Time of Transformation (New Dynamics for Social Responsibility)*. Hampshire, England: Palgrave-Macmillan, pp. 72–74.

Price Waterhouse Cooper 2014. *The Future of India: The Winning Leap.*

Ross, John 2004, *Understanding the Demographic Dividend.* Washington, DC: Policy Project, Futures Group.

Statistical Yearbook for Asia and the Pacific 2014, ESCAP, United Nations, 2014.

The Global Innovation Index 2014: The Human Factor in innovation, Cornell University, INSEAD and WIPO, Fontainebleau, Ithaca, and Geneva, 2014.

Thomson, Andrew 2008. 'Exploring the Relationship Between Higher Education and Development: A Review and Report' Guerrand-Hermes Foundation for Peace, September.

Tilak, Jandhyala B.G. 2003b. "Higher Education and Development" Paper presented at a International Seminar: University XXI, Brasilia, Brazil, 25–27 November.

Tilak, Jandhyala B.G. 2013a. 'Higher Education in the BRIC Member-Countries: Comparative Patterns and Policies', *Economic & Political Weekly* 48(14): 41–47.

Tilak, Jandhyala B.G. 2004. 'Absence of Policy and Perspective on Higher Education', *Economic and Political Weekly* 39(21), 2159–64.

Tilak, Jandhyala B.G. 2003a. "Higher Education and Development in Asia", *Journal of Educational Planning and Administration,* Vol. XVII, No. 2, (April), pp. 151–173.

Tilak, Jandhyala B.G. 2005. "Post-Elementary Education, Poverty and Development in India" University of Edinburg, Centre for African Studies, Working Paper Series, No. 6, November.

Tilak, Jandhyala B.G. 2013b. 'Introduction' in Tilak, Jandhyala B.G. ed., *Higher Education in India: In Search of Equality, Quality and Quantity; Essays from Economic and Political Weekly*, New Delhi: Orient Blackswan Private Limited, pp. 1–18.

Varghese, N.V. 2013. 'Private Higher Education: The Global Surge and Indian Concerns', in IDFC Foundation *India Infrastructure Report 2012: Private Sector in Education* New Delhi: Routledge, pp. 145–156.

Whalley, John and Xiliang Zhao 2010. 'The contribution of human capital to China's economic growth' Working Paper 16592, Cambridge: National Bureau of Economic Research. December.

World Bank 2002. 'Constructing Knowledge Societies: New Challenges for Tertiary Education', Washington, D.C.: World Bank.

Xue, Lan 2006. *Universities in China's National Innovation System* Paper prepared for the UNESCO Forum on Higher Education, Research and Knowledge, November 27–30.

4

Globalization and Emergence of the Private Sector in Higher Education: China and India

Kavita A. Sharma

Introduction

The imperatives of globalization have led to an accelerated demand for higher education, especially since economic development and higher education have been inextricably linked. India and China are the two most populous countries of the world with completely different forms of governance. They present interesting synergies and challenges. Both have young populations, but the average age of China's population is higher than India's. By 2035, China's population is expected to skew heavily towards older age groups, while India's largest cohorts will be in the age groups below 50 years. This will have varied implications for employment in the two countries. As China's rapidly ageing population increases it will lead to economic constraints while India's will crest around 68 per cent in 2035, the year that India will surpass China on this statistic, and then go onto a decline slowly.[1]

Traditionally, higher education has been a contested site as it is the most affected by national interests. In the nineteenth century, higher education was seen as the pursuit of knowledge which was necessary for the well-being of a society. The purpose of higher education was essentially to produce highly cultivated people who would provide leadership to the society. Industrialization, globalization and the development of Information and Communication Technologies have led to a post-industrialized, networked society where economic development is linked to knowledge. The emphasis on higher education has consequently shifted from cultivation of the mind to skill development. Higher education institutions are expected to adapt to the rapidly changing world as the corporate vocabulary of effectiveness, efficiency, outcomes and quality has entered their discourse. Reforms have been proposed and implemented all over the world in higher education keeping these in mind. Every nation has responded in different ways to the challenges of globalization depending on their political regimen, economic structure and cultural traditions. In addition, there are specific issues at the national, regional and local levels which result in tensions between the local and the global.

With the linking of higher education to economic development, there is a move towards 'massification' of higher education and eventually its universalization as it is perceived that higher education leads to better paying jobs and everyone wants to take advantage of it. Questions have therefore arisen about the employability relevance and the quality of higher education. The need to simultaneously expand so that there is an increase in access and equity, and at the same time tackle the issues of relevance and quality by upgrading existing institutions, has put a strain on the resources available for the public funding of higher education[2]. The consequence is the emergence of the private sector in higher education and the prioritizing of subjects like engineering, medicine, management, media, law, applied sciences and technology together with the subjects related to the service industry and skill development. Social sciences and humanities are facing neglect which gets more and more emphasized as higher education moves to the private sector. Further, there is an acute need for research for knowledge formation in which boundaries between disciplines get blurred and its dissemination. All this means that the way we think of the organization, financing, governance structures and delivery systems of higher education has to be revisited with regard to state-funded institutions and the emergence of the private sector which has grown while policy for it has lagged behind[1].

How Did State Control of Higher Education Come About?

Many of the earliest universities of Europe, were the products of non-governmental initiatives during the second half of the Middle Ages. They were set up as autonomous institutions by royal or papal decrees. They had public orientation and were accountable to the secular or religious authorities. The distinction between the public and private spheres was not marked in medieval times and hence the dichotomy between public and private institutions was also less clear. It is only between the seventeenth and early twentieth centuries that the modern State expanded and included higher education as one of its functions.

The motivations for State control then were not very different from the motivations of the private sector today—politics and economics. The same factors that led to the 'nationalization' of higher education might end up in its privatization or at least in a mixed sector. The process began in the 1660s with the emergence of the modern State which came to regard the universities as the suppliers of qualified labour and so sought increasing control over them. As the functions of the State grew, new institutions were started by the State or the existing ones regulated so that they could be used to train new members of administration. By the nineteenth century, the autonomy of the university was impacted as the State sought to regulate the organization of the universities, syllabus, teaching staff and students. The growing role of government funding of universities has been accompanied by greater oversight on them. The ministries of education and similar public administrative structures exercise detailed control over university life. It has gradually become so overbearing that in the last decades of the twentieth century, this steady growth of persistent control of the State over universities started to be questioned. However, the situation is complex because in the process, the universities themselves have become strongly dependent on the State authorities at all levels—financial, administrative, educational and political. Freedom is frightening.

Hence a direct correlation can be seen between the expansion of the government's economic and social role and the government control over universities. The social welfare state required highly qualified people like teachers, social workers, doctors, engineers, accountants and others. This impacted syllabus formation and priority in the funding of types of programmes thus privileging some over others. It meant that expenditure on higher education became a budgetary and political priority and funding was made available for required skills and the scientific research required primarily for military, economic and social military purposes. It also led to the need for mass higher education as there was ever-increasing demand for the required workforce.

The pattern of higher education that developed in Europe with large scale funding was copied all over the world including India. With the rise of North America, the North American pattern which is different from the European model because of the development of a federal state and its limited role in the higher education is also beginning to emerge and is intensifying the debate on the State control of universities and the autonomy required in a democratized and globalized world[3].

In pre-independent India, a large number of institutions were established through private initiative but once Independence came, the State took over and this led to the demise of philanthropy in this sector. For obvious reasons, it chose to follow the European model and more particularly the British model. In this model, since the government had considerable control over institutions of higher education, the number of private institutions became insignificant. Higher education was seen as a State responsibility and as an instrument for training elites especially for the civil service and public administration. In pursuance of this ideology, private higher education was either prevented from being established or not allowed to continue to function.

The Growth of Private Higher Education in China

The large population of young people in both India and China and the spread of school education have meant that the demand for higher education has grown tremendously and the demand supply ratio has got highly skewed. But private education is not a new phenomenon. China has had a long history of private education from 521 B.C. onwards when Confucius established the first school, to 1949. However, by 1953, all universities and colleges in China were changed into public institutions within a central planning system. The Government began allocating greater resources to higher education, appointing university leaders, deciding enrolment numbers and other functions. In fact, intellectuals were regarded as enemies of the evolved people (Kormordy, 1982)[4]. The system of higher education was destroyed between 1966–76, the years of the Cultural Revolution. In the earlier part, the higher education institutions began to close down and only reopened in the early 1970s with much reduced enrolment compared to the pre-Cultural Revolution days. The admissions were no longer based on entrance examinations or academic records but individuals who had distinguished themselves in manual labour and possessed good political credentials were recommended by their work units. This led to a great decline in the quality of education.

China launched economic reforms in 1978 that were mostly in the domain of agriculture. During this period, higher education too was restored. In October, 1985, economic reforms with emphasis on urban areas were launched as China moved towards a market-oriented economy. Steps were taken to reform higher education[5]. In May 1985, a policy paper, 'The Decision to Reform the Education System' was issued. This marked the beginning of reforms in higher education in China.

Deng Xiaoping ushered in a new phase of 'socialist market economy with Chinese characteristics' in which socialism was married to market-oriented economy. As enrolment in higher education was low and also an acute shortage of skills was felt, it led to the realization that higher education needed to expand rapidly and even what was there had to be reformed as it did not produce the educational outcomes that could match the requirements of economic development. Consequently, the 'Outline for Education Reform and Development in China' was publicized in 1993 which led to the implementation of massive reforms. The new direction that the economy was given brought in its wake market mechanisms like diversification of financial resources, less administrative interference, the termination of assured jobs to graduates who had to then struggle to find jobs for themselves, and the emergence of private colleges[6].

Today, we live in a globalized world in which the essential mode of economy is capitalism that has taken various forms according to the needs of nation states. The Chinese economy is no different. It has led to Government controls being relaxed and new social groups have emerged including a new middle class. This has led to a surge in the number of private schools and universities. By the 1990s, there were about 1,300 private higher education institutions. By 2004, many of these institutions which had begun with a handful of students, had increased their enrolment to 3,000; the country had registered dozens of large private universities with more than 10,000 students each and more than a dozen had 20,000 to 35,000 students each.

Contradictions

There are many contradictions between intentions, policies and their implementation. These have led to tensions in higher education. For instance, in an effort to increase enrolment, the Government offered land to private institutions at rates much lower than market price; and tax breaks and even tax exemptions were given to private educational enterprises. This was because an effort was made to involve both public and private initiatives in the effort to expand higher education. Private institutions have been one of the fastest growing sectors in China, although they are unevenly distributed in different provinces. In spite of the support given by the Government for their establishment, there have been tensions between them and the Government because the Government wants to maintain tight control over them while private institutions demand greater autonomy.

Then there is the issue of faculty members. Initially, private universities were able to draw from the huge pool of teachers either currently active or retired from public institutions. Retired teachers from renowned public universities also helped to draw students. But the public sector itself has begun to privatize higher education by setting up 'second tier' colleges affiliated to the universities which utilize the resources of their respective universities, but charge tuition and other fees like the private universities. Teachers are assigned to teach in these colleges and are paid extra for it. Hence they see it as a way of increasing their personal income while the revenue of the public university also increases leading to a win situation for all. The public universities have also instituted reforms by which the pay is related to the workload. As a result, faculty members have had to double their teaching load to maintain their original salaries. The size of public universities too has doubled and in some cases trebled. This has resulted in a great shortage of teachers. It has shrunk the pool of faculty members available to private universities, creating an intense competition among them to recruit and retain teachers. Moreover, the teachers demand high salaries from private universities reducing their profit margins. Some find themselves spending about 80 per cent of their revenue on the salaries and allowances of their teachers. Private universities also try to build a loyal teacher pool by sending young teachers to undertake graduate studies, and rewarding meritorious teachers with recognition and higher emoluments. However, they find that once the teachers mature and gain experience, they move on to greener pastures.

On the one hand, faculty staffing is a challenge and on the other, students who pay high fees, demand quality education. Unlike earlier, private universities find it difficult to get away after making extravagant promises. This is because the source of students is dwindling because public universities as pointed out before have greatly increased their intake. Hence the private universities that had also increased their capacity to enrol students are now facing a reduced demand. Further the expansion in Chinese senior high schools has not kept pace with the capacities of the higher education institutions. This has shrunk the pool of students applying for higher education. In the 1980s and up to the early 1990s, 10–20 million students sat for the National University exams, of which only 4 per cent were accepted. Currently about 6 million appear in the exams of which approximately 50 per cent are accepted. This makes private universities resort to all kinds of tactics to recruit and retain students. Many universities spend upto 20 per cent of their revenue on advertisement and recruitment. Students, too, have become choosy. They do not accept all the claims made by private universities but visit campuses to see the facilities for themselves.

In order to get the requisite number of students to make the ventures viable, private universities exert pressure on their teachers to recruit students and retain them. Many students who join are actually not fit for higher education leading to a peculiar situation. Teachers may be dismissed because they are too good to teach slow students and have a higher standard of teaching. Such situations create unease among the faculty members exacerbating the faculty crisis.

Then, the private universities have an adversarial relationship with government officials and the public sector universities. Although the Government's avowed purpose is to encourage and support private universities, it has also strengthened its supervision and control over them. The Central and local governments with their emphasis on scrutiny, deny them the degree granting powers even after a decade or two of existence. This has relegated these universities to a second class status. They are also not given research funds by the Government and so are unable to improve their social recognition. In short, private universities cannot survive without the support of the Government.

A major issue relates to the ownership of private universities. As there is ambiguity over ownership and private property itself in China, the question of proprietary rights gets confusing and fuzzy. Further, education is seen as a 'public good' and hence it is emphasized that private educational institutions should not seek to make profits. However, the Government has had to bow to increasing pressure and revise its policies on Minban or people-run educational institutions. On December 20, 2002, the National People's Congress passed the 'Law for the Promotion of Minban Education' in which 'reasonable return on private education' was allowed. But what is 'reasonable' and how is it to be calculated—on the initial investment made by the investor or its current market price and other factors remains unclear..

The Ministry of Education was supposed to produce detailed guidelines for the implementation of this law by August 2003 but these came out only in March, 2004. The issue really boils down to control vs. autonomy. The private universities are under highly centralized control of the Government that sets strict quotas for enrolment in certain subject areas, approves their degrees and diplomas and can take away their degree granting powers at will. Another hugely debilitating measure is that private universities are allowed to admit students only after all public universities have finished their recruitment. Thus they get extremely substandard students but are evaluated as if they are equal to public sector universities. The tug of war between the Government officials and private universities thus continues. Currently, every year, one hundred private universities seem to be established and an almost equal number of them appear to close down. Some attempts are being made to establish accreditation bodies for these universities that would factor in the distinct role that they play. Hence, the dilemma is of not wanting to let go of control and yet finding it necessary to mobilize forces within society to participate in the offering of education to make China a knowledge society and a knowledge economy[7].

India

The situation in higher education is not very encouraging in India. While there has been a massive expansion of higher education after Independence, making it the third largest system after USA and China, it is highly inadequate in terms of access, equity and quality. Currently, it provides access to around 17–18 per cent of the relevant population (numbers vary) and efforts were being made to reach about 25–30 per cent by 2017. To do it in the public sector alone might be extremely difficult and so the private sector might need to be co-opted. This is because the financial requirement as estimated in the Twelfth Five year Plan is about 413,000 crore rupees. The number of seats that need to be created are 21 million and over 140 million children will need skill development. There is just no way in which public finance can meet this requirement, but the task has to be undertaken if economic development has to go forward.[8] It is also important to note that currently India spends about 1.1 per cent of its GDP on higher education while South Korea spends, over 2 per cent and USA over 4 per cent. Of course, there is a whole range of figures on how much countries spend on higher education, but the simple point is that India has to spend far more on higher education than public finance has the capacity to allocate.

In India, the strains on the system are more than evident as there are only a few research universities at the top and the bottom does not adequately fulfil the requirements of demand and so has little time to devote to relevance and quality. The skill formation is inadequate and too dysfunctional to meet the requirements of a growing and diversifying economy. While IITs and IIMs may be internationally competitive, they are only niche institutions which cater to a very small percentage of student population. One of the fundamental causes of the malaise is, perhaps, what Prof. Altbach points out when he says that the mass of institutions of higher education have no clarity of vision about their purpose and aim[9]. The universities are neither provided resources nor do they have the mandate to build a distinctive and innovative profile which is essential for successful academic systems. So they continue as an undifferentiated mass repetitively producing more of the same. If there was clarity on what different institutions are attempting to deliver, then their funding sources and patterns could also be diversified. We do not have that kind of luxury.

The accountability in the system is so diffuse and distributed that no one can be held responsible for delivery and outcomes. This leads to mediocrity. It is only natural because most academic arrangements in India have been derived from British colonialism and were not meant to be effective or to encourage quality. The most affected is undergraduate education as the affiliating system puts the undergraduate colleges under the universities with their highly bureaucratized and controlled environment. It impedes innovation as they have to follow the common centralized policies without any autonomy. The universities, in turn, receive their funding from the governments. So while they have formal autonomy, they too are basically under the control of central or state governments. Also, they have been politicized which makes them ideologically blinkered and contentious. All this has made issues of quality assurance very ambiguous.

The Emergence of the Private Sector

What has been the societal and systemic response to this situation? At least two things have happened. One is that it has led to the emergence of a very substantial private sector that has stepped in to absorb the rising demand for higher education especially in areas of professional and management education. The second is that the Government itself has realized that it will not be able to meet all the financial requirements of the demand and has tacitly recognized the need to involve the private sector. Therefore it has allowed elements of private education to enter the public sector universities and colleges through mechanisms like 'self-financing courses' that run concurrently with public funded programmes. Also, self-financing institutions have been affiliated to public universities and they now far outnumber the public funded colleges. Most of them are located in the southern states of India. Many private deemed universities have emerged which indicates that the governments seek private help and lacking a transparent policy or legislation have taken this route to enable private institutions to flourish. There are other groups of private institutions in the non-university sector that are run by private and corporate initiatives like NIIT and APTEC. By law, they cannot award degrees, but they attract students because of the quality and relevance of their programmes and training that they offer.

By the 1980s, the student preference started shifting to professional programmes over academic disciplines, particularly in areas related to engineering, medicine, management, computer applications and others because of economic and political factors. Finding a vacuum and sensing an opportunity, the private providers took to the professional sector in large numbers and did well. They were supported by an unarticulated paradigm shift in the Government policies. This can be seen from the various policy statements that emerged around this time.

The National Policy on Education, 1986, stated:

> Resources to the extent possible will be raised by mobilizing donations, asking the beneficiary communities to maintain school buildings and supplies of some consumables, raising fees at the higher levels of education and effecting some savings by the efficient use of facilities ... All these measures will be taken not only to reduce the burden on state resources but also for creating a greater sense of responsibility within the education system.[10]

The position was reiterated in 1992.

Among the first indications that the policy on private sector would reach the realms of implementation came in the recommendations of the Eighth Plan (1992–97) which stated that the opening of new universities and colleges should not be encouraged. Also it was clarified that private sector and voluntary agencies would be involved in the opening and running of higher education institutions with proper checks to ensure maintenance of standards and facilities. Higher education institutions were to be made as self-financing as possible. The protests of the academic community were muted by stating that the quality of education would not be compromised. Earlier, the Report of the CABE on Gnanam Committee (1992) had stated:

> It will also not be possible for the State Governments to find adequate resources to create Endowment Funds for each university. Universities however should make efforts to raise own resources but it must be ensured that there are no conditions attached like preference in admissions, etc. Raising of resources should not affect academic standards and universities should lay down guidelines for the same[11].

This position was not unique to India. It was in keeping with what was happening globally and had been stated by the International Commission for Education for the twenty-first century in 1996 in its report 'Learning the Treasure Within.' It was felt that since education had to be a lifelong process that was built upon a sound foundation of formal education, governments alone could not find the resources. Hence money had to be raised from the private source and also through communities and student fees[12].

In 1997, the Ministry of Finance in its White Paper on public subsidies called higher education a 'non-merit' good. This was significant because it could have had long term consequences for public financing of higher education as it made individuals the main gainers from it and hence not deserving of public subsidies. This is an old and continuing debate. If higher education is a 'public good' it must be completely supported by the government. It improves human capital, encourages civic involvement, and boosts economic development. The private good or "non-merit" counterargument is that higher education largely benefits the individual and therefore students should pay a significant part for their post-secondary education. Perhaps there is truth in both and the answer need not be an either/or proposition. In that case a policy in which both can co-exist can be formulated. This has not been done so far in the public domain as a national policy.

However, the Government has been more than aware of the resource constraints and tried to address the problem by introducing the Private Universities Establishment and Regulation Bill in August 1995 in the Rajya Sabha. It was referred to the Standing Committee for obtaining its views on involving the private sector. However, the Bill just faded away. Since the matter continued to be discussed at various forums, the HRD Ministry set up a core group in 1999 for their views and recommendations on various issues pertaining to higher education. Nothing came of it probably because it was politically contentious and the private sector too was very resentful of some of the provisions of the proposed bill like those pertaining to endowment fund, regulation by the Government bodies and free education to one-third of the students. The Birla-Ambani Report of 2001 also suggested the involvement of the private sector, minimal subsidies for higher education and the resources so saved be used for school education.

The Eleventh Plan had a massive increase in the outlay for education and several new initiatives were envisaged which would lead to a substantial expansion of higher education like the establishment of central universities, world class universities and colleges in every district. Even if it could all have been be implemented, it would still have required massive inputs from the private sector to meet the demand for higher education. The 12th Plan tried to consolidate but given the increase in secondary education, India's youthful demographic profile, and the existence of an already large private sector, a clear policy on private higher education and acceptance of public private partnership still had to emerge.

However, there is resistance to the idea of privatization among a vociferous and influential section of society which is a hindrance in formulating a concrete national policy towards private higher education and its role. The contention of this section is that since education has never been a commercial activity in this country, making it one is opposed to the ethos, tradition and sensibilities of the nation of India. But these contentions are not reflected in the actual practices. For example, medical care even more than education should be the responsibility of the Government, but the moment one is sick there is a rush for the best private nursing home. There is obviously some hypocrisy here which is evident in the education sector as well. Flourishing coaching academies, tutorial colleges and parallel colleges collect substantial fees for unregulated academic programmes and these are willingly paid. Fees are also willingly paid for the sought after schools and computer institutes but when it comes to formal higher education any fee increase meets with fierce resistance.

Early Private Higher Education in India

However, resistance to private education continues although it is resilient enough to persist and grow. Why is it so? After all, India has had a long experience in this area. In colonial times, institutions of higher education were started with little or no support from the Government. Socio-religious trusts, societies and even individuals took the initiative motivated by their ideals and philanthropy. The Sikhs in Punjab formed the Khalsa Diwan in 1873 which established Khalsa schools and colleges. Sir Syed Ahmad Khan founded the Mohammadan Anglo-Oriental College in 1877 which grew into Aligarh Muslim University in 1920. The Jamia Millia Islamia was founded by Dr. Zakir Hussain in 1920. The Arya Samaj founded a number of schools and the Anglo Vedic College in Lahore in 1886. The Deccan Education Society was founded in 1880 and started the Fegusson College. In Bombay, the Victoria Jubilee Technical Institute was founded in 1887 through local initiative. Dr. Annie Besant of Theosophical Society founded the Central Hindu College in 1909 which was handed over to Banaras Hindu University Society. She then teamed up with Pt. Madan Mohan Malviya to establish the Banaras Hindu University in 1917. In 1921, Gurudev Rabindranath Tagore started Viswa Bharti at Shantiniketan. Mahatma Gandhi was the motivating force behind the establishment of several institutions in the 1920s—Gujarat Vidyapeeth, Kashi Vidyapeeth, Tilak Maharashtra Vidyapeeth, etc.

The rulers of princely states too took keen interest in higher education and contributed to the establishment and development of universities like Mysore University (1916), Osmania University (1918) and Annamalai University (1929). Business houses too made their contribution to higher education and continued till much later after Independence although philanthropy in this field largely died out after 1947. The efforts of Jamshedji Tata led to the establishment of Tata Institute for Science now called Indian Institute of Science at Bangalore. Educational programmes initiated by G.D. Birla at Pilani in the early 1900s culminated in the establishment of the Birla Institute of Technology and Science, Pilani in 1964. B.M. Birla started the Birla Institute of Technology, Ranchi in 1955. Banasthali Vidyapeeth (1983), Thapar Institute of Engineering and Technology, Patiala (1985) and Bharti Vidyapeeth (1964) too are examples of private initiatives[13].

Contemporary Private Higher Education

Private education existed earlier too, and private higher education has emerged now; what is the difference between the two? Historically, private institutions were established as not-for profit institutions like the universities. However, the recent growth of private institutions are inevitably profit-seeking. Even when for profit institutions are not allowed, the private institutions are usually for profit whatever may be their claim to the contrary and the regulatory mechanism is not able to deal with them. Further, most private institutions are not universities but specialized institutions that provide higher training in some specific fields of study. Research, especially in basic sciences is usually weak in them and often non-existent because of the large outlay it demands. However, in recent times, attempts to gain legitimacy have prompted them to show some amount of research activity but it largely remains cosmetic because it is difficult for them to find philanthropic sources of funding and they have no access to public research funds. So whatever finances are required for research have to be cross-subsidized from teaching funds and this involves raising tuition fee, already high compared to public universities, to a point which is not a viable option. As the system matures, some amelioration may take place.

Right now, most private higher education institutions cater to undergraduate demand which satisfies the current needs of the labour market as this brings immediate returns. However, high-end programmes demand heavy financial outlay which in turn means very high fees. Since there are no takers for this, either the quality gets diluted or private education gets confined to the popular courses of social sciences, economics business, management and others.

The issue of quality becomes an urgent one for them since they find it hard if not impossible to compete in terms of fees with public institutions. Also these institutions face problems of getting good teachers. Most of them have to rely on part-time teachers from public universities or retired faculty members from these universities. The dearth of faculty members disturbs the teacher student ratio that further dilutes the quality. Further, when teachers from public institutions `moonlight' it creates tensions between the two sectors with its own consequences. Public angst too rises against them because lack of quality and high fees means that the employment returns do not match the individual investment and expectations.

Further, at the policy level, the expectations from private institutions are usually not met. Given the fact that they have more flexibility, it is expected that they would increase diversification both in terms of geographical reach and subjects taught being more responsive to labour market demands. This does not happen because the very nature of private institutions makes them gravitate to capital cities or major urban centres. And the subjects get confined to those that are popular because of market demand. In fact, it is the public institutions that are geographically diverse because of the involvement of local and regional authorities. They also have the wherewithal to innovate if they could only get out of their straitjackets.

But whatever may be the constraints on private higher education, the evidence seems to suggest that they are set to become a permanent feature of the higher education landscape. This is because higher education is likely to persist as an important priority in policy terms and yet, the Government may not be able to cope with its rising financial demands and expectations, and this will give a push to private higher education. There will also be financial challenges on how to expand the supply of higher education but these will be in both the public and the private sectors. Unless there is a policy that will take into its ambit the concerns of both the sectors, the likely response will be the strengthening of market mechanisms which can increase the unregulated growth of privateness in the system. The consequence will be commercialization of higher education and the victims will be the stakeholders—teachers, students and parents. Teachers will be underpaid and hired on contractual basis with their services being dispensed with during vacations. They will have career uncertainties. Students will not get quality education and parents will pay exorbitant fees in their quest for professional degrees for their wards. Hence it is vital to have a public policy with regard to private education in place to avoid the ills of commercialization. This will however be a complex and controversial issue especially in countries where private institutions have remained minimal or there are ideological issues and public sentiment to grapple with.

Since private education usually gets a boost because of massification, initially at least, it will tend to focus on absorption of unfulfilled demand but gradually these institutions may position themselves as high quality/high cost alternatives to mass/low cost public higher education. In the course of time they would not want to be seen as second choice institutions for those who could not get a place in the public sector institutions. In the post massification phase, the demand absorption pattern can also give way to niche institutions which present alternatives to mass higher education rather than reinforcing it.

Private institutions will gradually seek greater legitimacy. The first endeavour will be to strengthen their teaching mission both in terms of programmes and faculty staff. They will also start paying more attention to research. Up to now, the teaching element has been dominant, but they will focus on research for legitimacy. They will attempt to improve their academic pedigree with better qualified staff, increase the number of research centres affiliated to them and develop good post-graduate programmes. In addition they are also likely to develop good and strong student support mechanisms because both academic quality and students are equally important to them[14].

Models for Private Higher Education

Many models for private education are already available in the country. There are at least four distinct ones. One is the Manipal model where the approach is to provide access to students who can pay and who may not have got admission for various reasons in a public sector universities. Manipal Academy of Higher Education is a pioneering centre for self-financing higher education, managed and funded by private enterprise.

The second is the marketing model in which already existing institutions receiving aid from the government central or state are allowed to start some professional courses at the undergraduate and postgraduate levels on the self-financing pattern.

The third is the sponsoring model which is popular with the corporate sector in which it sponsors its managerial and executive personnel to enable them to update their skills and knowledge. For this they are attached to some leading institutions for a short period of training.

Finally, there is the franchising model in which self-financing institutions have to select courses designed by a university and follow the teaching as per norms prescribed by the affiliating university. However, these colleges do not receive grants from the governments. Guru Gobind Singh Indraprastha University, Delhi has a large number of privately managed self-financing courses in different professional fields such as engineering, technology, management studies, medicine, pharmacy, education, law and others are affiliated to it.

Governments will increasingly develop accreditation and evaluation mechanisms often as an instrument to curtail private institutions. This will gain relevance as for-profit institutions emerge as they are already doing in many countries of the world and even the not-for-profit ones behave like for-profit ones. Private institutions too will seek accreditation to legitimize themselves and proclaim their quality.

Need for Government Policy

The acceptance of private higher education will essentially depend on the role of the Government. The Government has to be clear, and build a national consensus on the issue. Right now there is divergence and the public perception is negative with fair justification. At the same time, paradoxically the private sector continues to grow while policy lags behind. Therefore, benign negligence of the private sector or allowing its covert entry will not do. If the Government needs the private sector for resource mobilization and its other strengths, it has to facilitate the private sector and see it as complementary to its task of discharging its responsibility of expanding the higher education base. If this is the perception, then potential private providers can be given facilities and some incentives. For this, the most important is appropriate legislation because it will embody the will of the State and bring about clarity on the rules of the game. It will save the private sector education from perpetual litigation and harassment. Security by legal action would constitute the first step in promoting quality private participation in higher education. Regulations implemented with integrity can lead to open and transparent policies that can attract big corporations with enough funds to establish quality institutions and staying power to not expect immediate returns.

Lacking a national legislation, many states have already enacted rules for the establishment of private universities sometimes they do so with disastrous consequences as in Chhatisgarh. But state legislation is not enough. The national will must be made clear through a national policy which should have basically three components: (i) promotion, (ii) facilitation and (iii) regulatory control. The promotional role needs policies that stimulate private efforts through expansion of higher education. Facilitation requires enacting of appropriate legislation and regulatory control is needed to ensure good quality in private institutions as well as to safeguard against any exploitation of the gullible public.

Conclusion

Chinese higher education desperately needs flexibility and creativity, and the full participation of society in its provision. It is recognized that putting in place a viable system of higher education requires the efforts of the whole of society, as well as government policies and legal support. All in all, the Chinese Government needs to exercise broad supervision but their priority should be to give private universities the autonomy to build their own niche and provide a rich array of services to society, based on the needs of the economy.

Right now, higher education in India also seems to be stuck in a quagmire. It is clear that India is affected by global trends but is unable to deal with them. If it has to meet the challenges, it has to systematically create an internationally competitive academic system. For this it will have to rise above ideological biases and politics to reform its outmoded structures of academic governance structures and delivery systems and build a national consensus by a continuous Centre-state dialogue on higher education both in the public and the private sectors. A tall order perhaps, but without it the Indian higher education system can deliver neither nationally nor compete globally.

Notes

1. www.rand.org/pubs/research_briefs/rb9598/index.1.html
2. Philip G. Altbach, *Tradition and Transition: The International Imperative in Higher Education,* Sense Publishers Netherlands, Jan. 2007, pp. 3–22. Also see Philip G. Altbach, *Global Perspectives on Higher Education: The International Imperative in Higher Education,* Sense Publishers: Netherlands, 2007, pp. 7–10.
3. Pedro Teixeira, "Mass Higher Education and Private Institutions", *Higher Education to 2030; Globalization,* Vol. 2, OECD, 2009, pp. 232–258.
4. *Change,* Vol. 14, No. 5 (July-August 1982) pp. 32–37. See also, Philinp G. Attkach, "The Giants Awake: Higher Education Systems in India and China", *Economic and Political Weekly,* Vol. XLIV, No. 23, June,6, 2009, pp. 39–57.
5. Edward J. Kormondy, "The People's Republic of China: Revitalizing an Educational System" *Change,* Vol. 14, No. 5 (July-August 1982) pp. 32–37.
6. Qiang Zha, "Diversification or Homogenization: How Governments and Markets have combined to (Re) Shape Chinese, Higher Education in its Recent Massification Process", *Higher Education,* Vol. 58, No. 1, July 2009, pp. 41–58.
7. The contradictions between a market oriented higher education and the socialist form of governance together with the highly centralized form of governance ingrained in the system, have led to an unequal system experiencing several strains but firmly tied to government control. Jing Lin, Yu Zhang, Lan Gao and Yan Liu, "Trust, Ownership, and Anatomy; Challenges Facing Private Higher Education in China," *The China Review,* Vol. 5, No. 1, Spring 2005, pp. 61–81. See also Li Feng Liang and W. John Morgan "Private Higher Education in China: Access to Quality Higher Education and the acquisition of Labour Market Qualifications by low income students", *Education, Knowledge and Economy,* Vol. 2, No. 1, March 2008, pp. 27–37. Ka Ho Mok, "Rising over Socialism and Global Capitalism: Changing education governance and social policy paradigms in post-Mao China", *Comparative Education,* Vol. 41, No. 2,

May 2005, pp. 217–242. Ka Ho Mok, "Globalization and Educational Restructuring: University Merging and Changing Governance in China", *Higher Education*, Vol. 50, No. 1 (July, 2005), pp. 57–88. Rui Yang, "Globalization and Higher Education Development: A Critical Analysis, *International Review of Education*, Vol. 49, No. 3/4, July 2003, pp. 269–291. Yuzhuo Cai, "Confronting the Global and the Local—A Case Study of Chinese Higher Education", *Tertiary Education and Management*, Vol. 10, No. 2, pp. 157–169.

8. *Twelfth Five Year Plan (2012–2017) Social Sectors*, Vol. III. Also, *Narayana Murthy Committee Report*, Planning Commission, New Delhi, 2012.
9. This has been the theme song of Philip Altbach. See Pawan Agarwal, *A Half Century of Indian Higher Education*, Sage, New Delhi 2012.
10. National Policy on Education as modified in 1992.
11. Report of the CABE Committee on Gnanam Committee Report, April 1992.
12. Jacques Delora, *Learning the Treasure Within*, UNESCO, 1996.
13. Kavita A. Sharma, *Sixty Years of the University Grants Commission: Establishment, Growth and Evolution*, New Delhi: University Grants Commission, 2013, pp. 9–12.
14. Pedro Teixera, "Mass Higher Education and Private Institutions", op cit., See also Daniel C. Levy, "An Introductory Global Review: The Private Fit to Salient Higher Education Tendencies", *WP* No. 7 September 2006.

5

The State in the Internationalization of Higher Education: India and China Contrasted

Sreemati Chakrabarti

Internationalization of higher education has at its crux access to global scholarship and cross-border exchange of knowledge. In operational terms, it involves student and faculty exchange, joint research projects, sharing of publications, information and data, and so forth. In the post-globalization era, its meaning and definition have expanded. Associated with soft power projection of states, with commercialization and political considerations, internationalization of higher education, in the present era, is seen from a wider perspective. Jane Knight, a leading scholar in this area has defined it as "the process of integrating an international, intercultural or global dimension into the purpose, functions or delivery of post-secondary education".[1]

The UNESCO (2006) gave the following definition: "It is higher education that takes place in situations where the teacher, student, programme, institution or provider and course material cross national jurisdictional borders. Cross-border education may include higher education by public or private and not-for-profit/for-profit providers. It encompasses a wide range of modalities in a continuum from face-to-face (taking various forms from students travelling abroad and campuses abroad) to distance learning (using technologies and including e-learning)". In the era of globalization, the need for advanced levels of education cannot be exaggerated as education levels determine a country's absorptive capacity that is capacities to adopt new technologies and develop them further. Education levels affect an individual's ability to deal with change, an important aspect in a globalized world that expects individuals to constantly adapt to new situations. Globalization also requires effective communication in terms of linguistic skills, technological skills and skills to deal with different institutions and cultures. "Unfortunately, higher education in most developing nations, points out Yibing Wang, has been ill-prepared for facing this challenge, and there is a lack of clear strategy and policy to deal with it due to historical, political, educational and cultural reasons or considerations".[2]

China's Reform era (1978 onwards) and India's Liberalization period (from 1991) have led to a massive growth in their higher education sectors. Expansion of the number of students desirous of higher education and establishment of a vast number of higher education institutions (HEIs) in both the countries was visible since the last decade of the twentieth century. Currently, in India 23 per cent of its college-age population are enrolled in HEIs (as per the latest information from the MHRD) and the goal is to reach 30 per cent by 2020. China, in 1978 had only 1.2 per cent and presently it has reached 30 per cent. The stated goal is to reach 40 per cent by 2020. Today, India and China lead the world in absolute number of students enrolled in HEIs. The numbers of HEIs in both the countries have grown phenomenally. Both nations and their governments are of the view that without a boost to the process of internationalization, the aim of becoming a 'knowledge economy' will not be achievable.

Prior to the 1990s, India's and China's records on higher education in general and with regard to internationalization, in particular, were more or less in India's favour. This had to do with the closed political system and a command economy in China's case and India's relatively open system. In the early post-Liberation period, China's higher education sector (like all other sectors) was under the complete domination of the Soviet Union. One outcome of this was that the number of comprehensive universities was reduced to 18 whereas specialized HEIs were set up in large numbers. In post-Independence India, only a few HEIs (IITs and IIMs) in the areas of engineering and management were established with foreign collaboration. Collaborations between Indian and foreign universities were few and far between in terms of student and faculty exchange, and joint research projects. Only a modest number of students and teachers (mostly in science and engineering) went abroad to study and teach. The Bilateral Cultural Exchange agreements signed between the Indian and foreign governments facilitated many of these student-faculty exchanges.

In the post-liberalization period, both India and China, like many other rapidly developing countries, began to restructure and develop their higher education systems to meet the needs of globalization and for their own growth. Internationalization was an obvious arena where new directions and developments were required. My main argument here is that while in China objectives have been identified, priorities and goals determined, the trajectory of higher education internationalization is visible. In India, even though the State has not lagged behind in stressing its importance, the uncertainties surrounding it are glaring. Much of the internationalization in India has happened through the non-State efforts. In China, the State is in almost complete control of the internationalization process whereas in India it remains in the fledgling form while the debates go on as there still prevail fears and apprehensions about internationalization.

China

The Cultural Revolution onslaught on college and university education had to be overcome. Guided by Deng Xiaoping's epigraph that education needs to be geared to face up to "modernization, the world and the future", the Chinese leadership began dispatching students abroad as soon as the reform era began. In July 1978. the Ministry of Education (MoE) came out with a document titled 'Report on Enlarging the Number of Overseas Students Dispatched Abroad' which stressed that students pursuing the natural sciences were to be given preference. While the number of Government-supported students going abroad increased each year, by the early 1980s, there were many students who were interested in studying abroad using their personal funds. In January 1981, the State Council approved the policy document 'Interim Provisions on Self-Funded Study Abroad'. After this a series of such policies were announced. As large numbers of students were returning to China after completing their studies abroad, the issue of the problems pertaining to them was put on the agenda. In 1981, the MoE came out with a 'Document on Proper arrangements of Overseas Returnees'. This urged work-units to keep in touch with students studying abroad, create conditions for them to return to be absorbed in suitable positions. In 1983, on the suggestion of a Chinese American physicist, the State Council established the Management and Coordination Committee of Post-Doctoral Scientific Research Stations. In 1986, the Government released the 'Provisional Rules on Overseas Students' and with this began the introduction of regulatory measures issued publicly towards strategies regarding education abroad. To ensure that Chinese students return to their homeland after completing their overseas education, policies were announced which included a 10 million Yuan research fund to help their work and employment in China. After the second phase of reforms following the Fourteenth Congress of the CPC, the principle of 'Supporting pursuing studies abroad, encouraging returning to the homeland and freedom to come and go' was upheld at the Third Plenum of the Congress in 1993. To implement this, the State Council in August 1992 released a policy document titled 'Notice Concerning People Studying Abroad'. In the 1990s too some more of such official guidelines were issued to keep track of students studying in foreign lands. Establishment of the China Scholarship

Council in 1996 was a landmark development in the State's support to students who wished to pursue education abroad but had limited resources.[3] The above policies and measures may not have achieved all the desired results, but they are clearly indicators of the efforts of the Chinese Government to support internationalization. After China joined the WTO, the MoE instituted the Supervision Office of Foreign Education within the Department of International Cooperation and Exchanges. In the first decade of this century too, a series of measures were taken up to ensure support to scholars going abroad.

International students coming to China in the Maoist era were overwhelmingly Chinese language and culture students. The Higher Preparatory School for Foreign Students, which is now called the Beijing Language and Culture University, was set up in 1962 catered to them. Most students came under arrangements between the Chinese Government and their governments. This remained the case in the early reform era where most students from abroad came under the Bilateral Cultural Exchange Programme. Sensing the demand from foreign prospective students who did not avail of the Government scholarships, the State Council in 1979 approved the 'Request for Instruction on the Changing Standards of the Self-Funded International Students'. This enabled self-supporting students to study in China. However, such students were studying the Chinese language through short-term courses. In 1980, the MoE issued the 'Notice on HEIs Offering Short-Term Chinese Training Courses for Foreigners'. This saw growth in the number of overseas students. In 1989, the MoE gave official approval to the provinces, autonomous regions and municipalities to admit and administer all self-funded foreign students. This was an important step towards granting autonomy to the HEIs. Also the number of students from the wealthy western countries, Eastern Europe and Japan started rising from the late 1980s. This obviously added to the income of universities and revenue for the governments.

After the second phase of reforms following the Fourteenth Congress of the CPC, not only have the number of foreign students in China increased phenomenally, but also they came in good numbers. It was not only for language training but also for studying medicine, engineering, business subjects, social sciences,, etc. Setting up of the China Scholarship Council, which now gives scholarships to students from more than fifty countries and adopting the Chinese language qualifying test (HSK) were two measures which further helped in getting many foreign students to China. As Perry and Kapur point out: "The PRC Government has made a major national investment, via its lavishly funded China Scholarship Council (CSC) in providing thousands of scholarships each year to send advanced graduate students and younger faculty abroad. In some cases CSC recipients enrol in multi-year foreign degree programmes; in other cases they simply spend a year of study and research at leading universities around the world. Many universities and local governments in China also offer substantial material incentives for overseas academic experience. Jilin University, for example, requires all its assistant and associate professors to spend at least one calendar year on a study or research programme abroad in order to become eligible for promotion to the next rank. Similarly, the municipal government of Shanghai offers a generous financial bonus to faculty members at the city's various universities upon their return from a year abroad on an approved research programme"[4] (Perry and Kapur, 2015).

In the 1990s, some regulations were passed which were to improve and modify earlier regulations to adjust to the large demand from foreign students and the equally strong desire of HEIs to admit them. A working strategy was announced which aimed at "expanding the scale, optimizing the structure, regularizing the administration and guaranteeing the quality".[5] In early 2010, the 'National Plan Outline for Medium and Long-term Education Reform and Development (2010–2020) was announced and as a follow-up on it the MoE issued a 'Plan for International Student Education in China' which mentioned that the goal was to make China the biggest destination of foreign students in Asia.

Faculty/expert collaboration has been more one-sided for obvious reasons. In 1979, the MoE invited 143 experts to China and that number has been increasing. According to Zhu and Lou, Deng Xiaoping in 1983 had stated that getting foreign experts to China was a long term strategy. "Under his instruction the Central Committee of the CPC and the State Council soon released several documents, stipulating explicitly the significance, emphasis, organization structure, working system, treatment, financial assurance and working procedure of foreign intellectual involvement. A leading group was set up and hosted a series of activities, and as a result, a considerable number of well known foreign experts were invited to China and an efficient working team of foreign intellectual support was formed." The subsequent[6] Five-Year Plan documents stressed the significance of foreign experts in China by stipulating policies and measures to make the efforts effective.

After China became a full member of the WTO a State Council document titled 'Regulations of the People's Republic of China on Chinese-Foreign cooperation in School Running' was released. In addition to the fact that all regulations must conform to the WTO rules, the document states the running of cooperative schools between Chinese and foreign collaborators have to "exclude education with special features such as compulsory education, military, politics and Communist Party schools and enrol mainly Chinese citizens with the objective of introducing high quality education resources...".[7] In the last two and a half decades, barring Tibet, Xinjiang and Qinghai, Chinese-Foreign cooperative schools were established in all the provinces of the PRC. Despite this expansion, this sphere of Chinese-foreign cooperation has many loopholes and problems. The two crucial problems are that they are too profit-driven and less-quality oriented.

China's association with the UNESCO began soon after it gained a UN seat in 1971. It set up in 1978 a National

Committee of UNESCO. However, cooperation has, by and large, been limited to attending meetings and conferences at the ministerial and senior official levels held in China or other countries. Two steps are significant in China-UNESCO cooperation. One is the setting up of an International Research and Training Centre in Baoding, Hebei Province, and the other is the Great Wall Scholarship which the MoE provides to UNESCO to subsidize the education of foreign students in China.

Establishing Confucius Institutes all over the globe is a master stroke of the Chinese leadership in the arena of internationalization of higher education. The Chinese National Office for Teaching Chinese as a Foreign Language (NOCFL), in short, Office of Chinese Language or Hanban was set up in 1987 which twenty years later led to the establishment of the Confucius Institute Headquarters in Beijing. The first Confucius Institute was set up in South Korea in 2004. Until now, there are nearly 300 Confucius Institutes spread across 88 countries. Their numbers are much more in the United States and Europe put together as compared to the total numbers in Asian and African countries. Confucius Institutes are located within universities but are independent entities. They offer training mainly in Chinese language and culture. Extending Chinese soft power is at the centre of the mushrooming of Confucius Institutes. Although there have been reports of late of the unease in some countries regarding the "hidden agenda" of the Confucius Institutes, yet their role in disseminating and popularizing Chinese language and culture cannot be ignored.

India

In India, internationalization of higher education remains a debatable issue and more so in the contemporary period of globalization. In the past, students, researchers and faculty have gone abroad to study and teach. Since the era of the Nalanda and Takshashila, scholars have come to India to learn. In the first few decades after Independence, Indians went abroad for studying subjects like medicine, engineering and law. Similarly, students, mainly from the developing countries, too came to India for higher education. A few universities have also had visiting faculty to teach highly- specialized subjects and foreign languages. All the IITs and two of the IIMs were set up with massive assistance from foreign countries. Foreign books and journals have always been on the reading list for undergraduate and advanced courses in almost all subjects. In the past, India did definitely benefit from international collaboration in selected areas of education. For instance, in the 1960s, collaboration in agricultural science and technology with the United States led to the 'Green Revolution'.[8]

India has the largest number of HEIs in the world. There are 18000 colleges and universities although the gross enrolment ratio is about 23 per cent. Brazil, China, Russia and Indonesia have a much higher ratio. The vast majority of these institutions are in the private sector.[9] (Samuel Paul, 2009). With Liberalization in the 1990s, internationalization was put on the agenda of higher education policies of the Government. According to one author, "Internationalization is a revolutionary development. The overall demand for higher and adult education, and professionally related courses, is increasing in most countries. There are several reasons for this: changing demographics, increased number of secondary school pass-outs, wish for continual learning, and the growth of the information technology. While demand is growing, the ability of the traditional institutions to satisfy this need is questionable."[10]

With the post-WTO/GATS regime in operation from the last decade of the 1990s, internationalization of higher education has become a multi-dimensional issue. With the huge demand for higher education from the massive middle-class which emerged as a result of rapid economic growth in many developing countries, the developed countries have found an opportunity to sell higher education. Similarly in India, the private sector has found a new arena for commercial activity. In India, the internationalization project is in the midst of debates and controversies.

Sunita Shrivastawa writing on this subject says that in the Indian context, globalization of higher education is not to be confused with internationalization. "Globalization of Indian higher education involves a super nationalism that straddles national boundaries, ignoring cultural identity. Technology often goes hand in hand with globalization, magnifying the threat. In contrast with globalization, internationalization of higher education recognizes the nation and describes a process of interchange of higher education between nations. It involves partnership between nations, between national systems and between institutions."[11]

In India's case, much of the internationalization that has happened has been in the non-governmental sector. Although the private sector has entered the higher education arena in a big way, yet many would argue that the Indian private sector has done little to either improve the quality of education or make it more accessible to the less privileged. Samuel Paul suggests seven modes of internationalization that are pertinent in the Indian context. They are: 1. Scale up the movement of students to foreign countries for higher studies. 2. Facilitate the participation of students in the distance education programmes of foreign universities (on-line learning). 3. Permit foreign universities to establish branch campuses in India to offer educational programmes. 4. Encourage foreign universities to offer joint programmes in collaboration with Indian universities on a much larger scale. 5. Award contracts to reputed foreign universities to collaborate in the creation of world-class universities in India. 6. Make our top universities/institutes a destination for foreign students on a large scale. 7. Encourage Indian institutions to set up campuses/ collaborations in other countries to meet the growing demand for higher education.[12]

Taking these seven as the objectives of the Indian higher education which are required to fit into an internationalized and globalized system, we find that the efforts of the Indian State have been rather limited and more so in comparison with the Chinese. In the mid-1990s, the University Grants

Commission(UGC) took the first step to look into the issue. A Study Group was formed to look into the various aspects of internationalizing Indian higher education.

The Association of Indian Universities (AIU) held round-table meetings first in the University of Mysore in February 2001 and next year in Guru Nanak Dev University in Amritsar. The recommendations came to be known as the 'Mysore Statement'. Both these round-tables undermined the importance of India's soft power projection and stressed the need for India becoming a knowledge society. The UGC in its Tenth Plan (2002–07) document laid emphasis on internationalization and as a follow-up measure, the UGC set up an Expert Committee and later a Standing Committee for the Promotion of Indian Higher Education Abroad gave its report in January 2004. The National University of Educational Planning and Administration (NUEPA) also organized a National conference in New Delhi in August 2004 where all aspects relating to internationalization were deliberated upon.[13]

In the year 2007, the University Grants Commission (UGC) came out with a document which was on: "Relevant Issues and Recommendations of Regional Conferences of the Vice-Chancellors" and based on a 'National Conference on Development of Higher Education for Expansion, Inclusion and Excellence'. The 44 pages of this document consists of about 3.5 pages on internationalization. While discussing regulation of foreign universities, it says: "Developing countries are now seen as a huge market for higher education and foreign universities from other countries are competing (with) each other to increase their market share. As the demand for opening the higher education sector in India for international service providers is increasing, the issue of providing appropriate regulatory framework for international education providers is under consideration of the Government. An effective regulatory mechanism is required to ensure quality higher education with equity and accountability." It goes on to add that the important issues to be considered are: 1. A regulatory framework for effective monitoring of international service providers regarding entry conditions, admission and fees and quality assurance. 2. Possibility of joint degree/collaborative programmes. 3. Mode of these programmes.

As late as in 2007, the debate and discourses on these issues go on and no concrete policies emerge. In the year 2010, the Government introduced the Foreign Educational Institutions (Regulation of Entry and Operations) Bill in the Parliament. As it did not get sufficient support in Parliament, it lapsed.

If one takes a look at the Annual Reports of the Ministry of Human Resource Development (MHRD) "International Cooperation" gets very little space. Take for instance, the 2013–14 Annual Report and just about half a page is devoted to it. What is only mentioned is that with fifty-one countries, India has entered into Educational Exchange Programmes or has MoUs. These envisage cooperation through initiatives which include exchange of scholars/students/researchers; sharing of information/publications; organizing joint seminars/ workshops /conferences; working towards mutual recognition of qualifications; and developing institutional linkages. Annual Reports do talk about the cooperation through the UNESCO, but most of the activity is limited to senior officials attending conferences and meetings abroad.

In the year 2013, the Central Government launched the *Rashtriya Uchchatar Shiksha Abhiyan* or the National Higher Education Mission. The 10–point 'Objectives' of the Mission clearly indicate the urgent need for India to revamp its higher education sector, but there is no mention of internationalization except the point number 4 which says that there is the need to "enable conversion of some of the universities into research universities at par with the best in the world". The MHRD in association with the Tata Institute of Social Sciences spelt out a comprehensive policy for the Indian State through this mission. The document, which has more than 200 pages (including 180 pages of text and annexures) devotes just about 10 pages to internationalization. It defines internationalization "as the process of integrating an international, intercultural or global dimension into the purpose, functions or delivery of higher education at the institutional and national levels". In the first part it gives an eight-point rationale for internationalizing Indian higher education. They are: Enhancing Capacity and Efficiency, Improving Standards and Quality, Competing in the Global Market, Shaping International Relations, Establishing a Regional Identity, Shaping India's International Reputation as a central node of an Ever-expanding Network of Knowledge and Training, Alleviation of Faculty-Crunch, Ease of Initiating Process as Government funding would be minimal. Looking at the current scenario, it states that "attitude towards internationalization has suffered a decline in the years since". The new economic realities of India will deter foreign institutions to fund India's HEIs, but many less developed countries may prefer to partner India for joint endeavours. The 'Current Challenges' this document lists are lack of: Data, Awareness of the International Scenario, Infrastructure, Clarity in Policy formation and Anticipation of Global Developments. The last but one challenge sums it up all: "While certain policies regarding Internationalization of higher education are embedded in long-delayed legislations (like the Foreign Education Providers Bill) it is still imperative for a broader policy framework to be put into place regarding all the above points...". As for 'Future Directions' the suggestions made are, among others, the need for a detailed survey to assess Student Flows, Investment and Understanding different markets, avoid administrative delays in issuing visas, etc., develop infrastructure at the university level like better hostels, support staff and assistance cells. It also suggests Twinning Programmes through creation of joint curricula, joint degree programmes and sharing of academic resources as well as Student-Faculty Exchange programmes. Offering English language teaching for students coming from non-English speaking countries is also mentioned as an important measure. The concluding comment here is that "while the current scenario concerning internationalization of higher education in India shows it to be an area ripe with opportunity, it is also clear that without a speedy, yet properly thought out policy formulation and implementation, India may yet miss out on capitalizing on it". A recent development geared towards promoting internationalization is the Global Initiative of Academic Networks or GIAN. The Governments of India and the United States have pledged to collaborate to facilitate short-term teaching and research programmes by upto one thousand U.S. academics in the Central Government funded Indian universities. This appears to be a worthwhile project and Modalities are being worked out by the MHRD but there are some "doubts or perhaps lack of clarity about the purpose and scope of GIAN."[14] GIAN is still at an initial stage.

In comparison with the State's role in China, India's has been neither extensive not intensive as the above discussion shows. Nothing like the Confucius Institutes is on the anvil. Here one needs to mention that the Indian Council for Cultural Relations (ICCR) has made its presence felt abroad and has a role in promoting Indian culture through education. Appended to the Ministry of External Affairs it has funded many international scholars specializing in Indian studies through fellowships. Scholars specializing in Indian culture and different fields of the social sciences have been doing useful research on India. ICCR has also established 108 Chairs of Indian Studies in universities abroad.[15] ICCR's efforts and achievements, however, can in no way be compared to the Confucius Institutes. They have limited visibility.

Conclusion

Only in the past two and a half decades has internationalization of higher education received so much prominence both globally and in the two States under study. It may be a little too early to judge if the desired goals have been reached or are reachable any time soon. Perry and Kapur point out: "The only aspect of international education where India is edging out China is in cross-border delivery of education services... the emergence of MOOCs—massive online open courses... is a potential game-changer in higher education... This is one instance where China appears handicapped relative to India due both to its comparatively low level of English language competency and to the extensive internet firewalls which make accessing these courses more difficult for prospective students in the PRC."[16] In China, the commencement of the Reform era (post-1978) saw the State's active participation in the higher education sector in general and also in its internationalization. With the advent of globalization and a more liberal economy in the 1990s, China's efforts on this score have doubled and positive results were visible. The State in China has been more than visible in this endeavour. In India, it was taken up at the governmental level only in the mid-1990s with the UGC setting up a Study Group. After that, a series of round table, meetings, conferences and so forth have been held, but very little follow-up action is visible. As far as the Indian State is concerned, the entire issue still remains in the realm of debates. One can easily argue that this is so because the natures of the two States are fundamentally different. China is a one-party authoritarian state where the leadership has limited accountability whereas India, a multi-party democracy, has to factor in many issues before formulating a policy that has the possibility of becoming controversial. Questions of state sovereignty, culture, equity and commercialization are related to higher education internationalization. One can make a counter-argument here: has China lost out on any of these in the internationalization process?

Notes

1. Jane Knight, *Higher Education in Turmoil: The Changing World of Internationalization*, Sense Publishers, 2008.
2. Yibing Wang, "Internationalization of Higher Education in China: A Practitioner's Reflection, *Higher Education Policy*, December 2008, Vol. 21, Issue 4, pp. 507-08.
3. Hong Zhu and Shiyan Lou, "Internationalization of Higher Education" in *Development and Reform of Higher Education in China*, 1992, Chandas Asian Studies Series, p. 192, cited in pp. 106-09.
4. Devesh Kapur and Elizabeth Perry ,"Higher Education in China and India: The Role of the State" (Paper for volume on The Changing Role of the State in Asia: Comparative Perspectives), January, 2015.
5. Hong Zhu and Shiyan Lou, ibid., p. 114.

6. Ibid., p. 124.
7. Ibid., pp. 125-26.
8. Prabhakar J. Lavakare, "Does India Have an International Higher Education Strategy?", *University World News*, Global Edition, Issue 276, June 15, 2013.
9. Samuel Paul,"Internationalization of Higher Education: Strategic Implications", *Economic and Political Weekly*, Vol. 44, Issue 9, February 28, 2009.
10. Subrata Kumar Mitra, "Internationalization of Education in India: Emerging Trends and Strategies" *Asian Social Science*, Vol. 6, No. 6, 2010, p. 5.
11. Sunita Shrivastawa, "Globalization and Internationalization of Indian Education", *Shodh, SameekshaaurMulyankan*, (http:// ssmrae. com/ admin/ images/244cdf2afb, pp.265-66.
12. Samuel Paul, op. cit., p. 39.
13. Kavita A. Sharma, *Internationalization of Higher Education: An Aspect of India's Foreign Relations*, Gyan Publishing House, 2008, pp. 65-66.
14. Pushkar, "Some Fresh *Gian*: Can India support a Global Network of Academics to Teach in its Universities?", *Indian Express*, February 18, 2015, (from 2016 some universities have invited foreign faculty for delivering lectures).
15. Cited by Eldho Mathews, "Where is India Heading?", *The World View*, September 25, 2014.
16. Kapur and Perry, op. cit., pp. 25-26.

6

Hitting a Glass Ceiling Soon? A Preliminary Assessment of China's Higher Education Development

Yang Rui

Introduction

During the past three and a half decades, China has made some remarkable achievements in its higher education development, evidenced especially in scientific publications and sheer numbers of graduates. While such progress has been widely acknowledged, the assessment of the future development of China's higher education is not an easy task. To some, Chinese universities are leaping ahead to join the distinguished league of the world's leading universities (Morgan, 2011). On a trajectory to become "world-class" (Marginson, 2011), China's high-flyers challenge Western supremacy and will gradually eclipse the Western university system (Healey, 2012). For instance, Professor Richard Levin (2010), former President of Yale University, warns that China's top universities could soon rival Oxford, Cambridge and the Ivy League. To others, Chinese universities still lag far behind the best in the West (Mohrman, 2005). A kind of "glass ceiling" is to be reached soon (Altbach, 2010). China's notion of "world-class" status has been largely imitative rather than creative. Pumping resources into universities will lead to diminishing returns as Chinese culture and practices will act as a brake to the pursuit of academic excellence.

People are kept informed about such over-generalizing views by both the media and scholarly works. While both views cite culture as the reason, neither of them is cultural enough. They are easy-minded judgements resulting from a shortage of the intimate knowledge of the Chinese system. With its strong traditions in higher learning that are fundamentally different from the Western, China faces consistent tensions with the contemporary dominant Western university model. Integrating its cultural roots and heritages with Western higher education values has remained unfinished (Yang, 2013). Based on the author's longstanding professional observation, this chapter assesses China's higher education development. After reporting some recent developments in China's higher education, it shifts its focus to the cultural meanings of and major challenges for higher education development in China. Aiming to form a fuller assessment of China's higher education development from a cultural perspective, it looks at how China indeginizes the Western concept of a university, and questions how far Chinese universities could move within their current development model. In particular, it attests Altbach's judgement that a kind of "glass ceiling" is to be reached soon by Chinese universities.

Recent Developments

Since the late 1970s, China's higher education has made some impressive progress. Admission has expanded dramatically since 1999. China's higher education system has become the world's largest in terms of sheer numbers of teachers and students. By 2013, 34.6 million students enrolled in China's 2,491 regular and 297 adult higher education institutions, with a gross enrolment rate of 34.5 per cent. Annual postgraduate admissions reached 611,400, with 540,900 and 70,500 respectively at Master's and doctoral levels and a total of 179,400 at-school postgraduate students. Teaching and administrative staff members reached 2,296,300 with 1,496,900 full-time teachers and a student-teacher ratio of 17.53:1. There were 718 private higher education institutions, enrolling 335

Master's, 3,616,400 undergraduate and 1,958,500 associate degree students (Ministry of Education, 2014).

As for research, especially in science and engineering fields, China's progress has been formidable. China is now the world's third largest producer of peer-reviewed research articles after the European Union and United States. According to Science and Engineering Indicators 2014 published by the US National Science Foundation, out of the world's 827,705 articles published in 2011, researchers in the combined 28 European Union countries produced 254,482 articles (31 per cent), the United States 212,394 (26 per cent), China 89,894 (11 per cent) and Japan 47,106 (6 per cent). Chinese science is clearly on the rise. China is pushing hard to increase its share of global research and development (Kigotho, 2014). Its output has surged during the past decade. The number of papers authored by Chinese scientists grew at an average of more than 15 per cent annually during 2001–11, rising from 3 per cent of global research article output to 11 per cent over the decade (Morrison, 2014).

China's progress has also resulted from a series of policy choices. Since 1978, establishing closer links between higher education and the market has been a prominent reform orientation. The Program for Education Reform and Development in China was initiated in 1993. The *Higher Education Law* (effective as of January 1999) stipulated decentralization in the Chinese system. The rapid expansion of higher education since 1999 further accelerated this trend. China's policies aim at both qualitative and quantitative developments in higher education. Since the 1990s, the Chinese Government launched the '211 Project' (1995) and '985 Project" (1998) in the quest for world-class universities. A handful of universities were selected to invest focally. Such projects represent the most ambitious goal of the Chinese Government in higher education development since 1949.

At certain stages, China's strategies have been effective. In the 2014 edition of QS University Rankings: BRICS, Chinese universities take 71 of the top 200 spots, including six of the top 10—convincingly positioning China as the current higher education leader within the competitive BRICS set. According to the latest Academic Ranking of World Universities (2014), China has 3, 3, 6, 13 and 7 positions respectively in the top 101–150, 151–200, 201–300, 301–400 and 401–500, featuring 32 times in the top 500. With such success, there has been evident pride in the idea that Chinese universities are not willing to assume that Western models define excellence and the related notion of the Chinese idea of a university (Yang, 2010). Discussions have started on whether or not there might be an emerging Chinese model of the university (Zha, 2011; Li, 2012; Postiglione, 2014).

China's achievement appears even more remarkable when compared with other non-western societies. A modern Western-style higher education system has been well established. It is a combined effect of China's many factors including its strikingly different higher learning traditions, chequered history of transplanting foreign education patterns, already well-established modern western-styled higher education system, remarkable economic growth in recent decades, and its tremendous talent pool. It is also a result of the past and the contemporary and the local and the global. However, most existing studies only look at one dimension of the studies. Researchers often see only certain aspects of highly complex issues. In particular, although universities are cultural institutions and China is especially rich in higher learning traditions, a cultural perspective is usually lacking in assessing China's higher education development. With its true meaning lying at the possibility of offering an alternative to the Western model, China's experience is indeed interesting to observers.

Two Systems

Higher education is deeply rooted in culture. Human civilizations of diverse regions of the world have had their various higher learning traditions. During its history going back thousands of years, China developed its rich traditions in higher learning that contrast sharply with those in the

West. Ancient Chinese higher learning institutions appeared in the Zhou Dynasty (1046–256 BCE). The famous Jixia Academy or the Academy of the Gate of Chi (*Jìxia Xuegong*, 稷下学宫) was established twenty years before the Platonic Academy in Greece (Hartnett, 2011). As Hayhoe writes:

> Traditional Chinese higher institutions can be traced back as early as the Eastern Zhou dynasty (771–221 B.C.). By the Tang Dynasty (618–907 A.D.) there was a whole range of higher institutions, headed by the Guo zixue (School for the sons of the Emperor) and the Tai xue - (often translated university) which took major classical texts of the Confucian school as their curricular content. There were also professional schools for law, medicine, mathematics, literature, calligraphy, and Daoist studies…In the later Song Dynasty (960–1279 A.D), the Confucian classics were reordered to form a knowledge system that had to be mastered by all aspiring to become scholar-officials in the imperial civil service. (Hayhoe, 1989, p. 54)

Chinese ancient education focused on knowledge of human society, with its central focus on political utility defined by the ruling class. China's classical higher learning featured a Confucian approach to scholarship with emphasis on connectedness and integration between theory and practice, fact and value, individual and community, institution and political-social-natural context (Hayhoe, 2001). Aiming at a close integration within a meritocratic bureaucracy that entrusted governance to those who could demonstrate their knowledge through written examinations, the tradition portrays the unique Chinese way of thinking about individuals, society and nature as well as the relations between them. Higher learning was to prepare would-be officials for the State. Higher learning institutions were a subsidiary body of the bureaucratic system. As part of the ruling system, they neither could nor attempted to go beyond the imperial framework. Even private institutions set their eye only at the imperial examination in the hope of winning an official rank (Zhang, 2009).

Chinese higher institutions did not have the Western-style autonomy and academic freedom. There was no institution that could accurately be called a university (Hayhoe, 1996). Higher institutions were loyal servants of the emperor. Chinese institutions were highly reliant on their relations with the ruling elites. The Imperial Examinations (*ke ju*, 科举) and the Academies (*shu yuan*, 书院) were key elements of ancient Chinese higher learning. The former began to take form around 400 C.E. and reached its full institutional development in the Tang dynasty (618–907 C.E.). During the Song (960–1279 C.E.), it crystallized into patterns that were to last right up to 1911. The latter took their definitive forms in the Song dynasty, as what had been originally libraries or centres for scholarly discussion. They provided a structured learning environment that was separate from yet interacting with State institutions associated with the civil service examination system. Such academies may have been a close parallel to the medieval universities of Europe (Hayhoe, 1989).

Lacking interest in seeking knowledge for its own sake, traditional Chinese higher education placed its central focus on utility in the terms of the ruling class. Some Sinologists stress the private nature and freethinking atmosphere of the academies (se, for example, Hayhoe, 1989). Yet, the academies did not always maintain those features. Their longstanding historical development bore a marked brand of ideological and financial control by the government. They focused initially on exploring Confucianism and promoting personal intellectual development than training government officials, with operating funds coming mainly from private sources. They became prosperous through winning recognition and financial support from the Song rulers. The government then further extended its control via donations of books and land. With gradual loss of independence from the government, the academies became a major part of the government education system, and trained many officials during the Southern Song dynasty (1127–1279). They were integrated into the government school system from the Yuan to the Qing dynasties. By the Qing dynasty (1644–1911), their major aim had turned to preparation for the imperial examination in the hope of winning an official rank (Zhang, 2009).

The Chinese tradition therefore contrasts markedly with medieval universities which were autonomous corporations of students and masters, governed by internal rules set by the academic community itself and protected from the outset by the papal bull issued by Pope Gregory. They were self-financing, depending either on their properties or on contributions from students for their income. They were small, independent institutions catering to the elite and governed by their own members, who elected a rector (Mora, 2001). Compared with the European curriculum that was featured by a hierarchical structure of knowledge and a dualism in epistemology and value neutrality, traditional Chinese scholarship was more fluid and less absolute in the lines it drew to separate itself from the natural environment, the political system, and religious authority (Hayhoe, 2001).

What is now described as the "global research university" is rooted in the universities established in Europe during the Middle Ages. The model was profoundly shaped by nineteenth century Germany and twentieth century America and spread around the world both through colonization and the emulation of its scientific achievements and contribution to nation building. China began to experiment with such universities in the late nineteenth century, with its first modern institution established in 1893 (Kirby, 2012). Attempts to indegenize the Western idea of a university since then have never stopped. Such efforts succeeded in varying degrees at various levels (Yang, 2011). Achievements were most evident at the individual level typified by Cai Yuanpei. Institutional success was exemplified by the National Southwestern Associated University (April 1937–May 1946) during the Second Sino-Japanese War. At the system level, the period of 1911–27 witnessed real efforts to set up a "university" in the sense of the defining values of autonomy and academic freedom, due mainly to the lack of a strong Central Government (Hayhoe, 1996).

The markedly different cultural roots and heritages have led to continuous conflicts between the traditional Chinese and the imposed Western ideas of a university. Modern Chinese universities have their institutional establishments based on Western values on the one hand and another system supported by traditional culture on the other. The two systems often do not support each other. Instead, constant tensions between them reduce the efficiency of university operation, and China's unique traditions have become a problem instead of an asset in the modernization of higher education. The two systems have never been on equal footing either. Today, Western models still influence the direction of change in Chinese institutions of higher education. Chinese universities look to the most elite Western counterparts for standards, policy innovation and solutions to their own development problems. The merging of Chinese and Western ideas of a university remains an unfinished business. China's emphatic determination to separate the advanced knowledge of Western countries from "decadent ideas" and a "bourgeois way of life" has overtones of the formula devised in its early modernization efforts: "Chinese learning as the substance, Western techniques for their usefulness" (Ayers, 1971). The disaggregation of Western culture into positive and negative elements remains arbitrary. China's policies continue to demonstrate prioritized economic considerations in higher education reforms (Sigurdson, 2004), leaving knotty issues of culture and values aside.

The co-existence of the two systems has significant cultural implications for the meaning of internationalization in China. In the past two decades or so, internationalization has been high on agenda at institutional, national, regional and international levels. Different perspectives have been adopted to examine the internationalization of higher education, and various understandings of the term abound with diverse emphases and approaches. The most cited definition was developed by Jane Knight (Knight & de Wit, 1995; Knight, 2008), based almost exclusively on Western experience. To non-Western societies, modern universities are an imported concept (Altbach, 2001). The so-called "international" perspective was imposed on them from the outset. What is lacking in the service of their higher education to their nation-building is an appropriate combination of the "international" and the local. Within the contemporary context of Western dominance, the internationalization of higher education necessarily touches upon the longstanding issues of and tensions between Westernization and indegenization. This is particularly true in China, where the oldest modern university was only founded in the early 1890s. Chinese higher education has been featured by Western models practicality fused with its Confucian virtues, operating fundamentally within the traditional mode of thinking, with the Western concept of the modern university taken by the Chinese for its usefulness. This is a stiff mix that has rarely been questioned thoughtfully, although there have always been attempts to indigenize the Western idea of a university started since the nineteenth century (Yang, 2013).

For China, the coexistence of two powerful systems of strikingly different Western and traditional Chinese cultural values proves an extremely tough challenge. While the choice for having both at the same time appears to be the only reality for the Chinese, the two systems do not tolerate each other easily. Chinese traditional ways of thinking have survived dramatic social and cultural changes in China's modern history, and remained deeply rooted in the Chinese society. Their impact on contemporary Chinese higher education is amazingly profound. The clash between the two traditions forms the most fundamental cultural condition for China's contemporary higher education development. It is a spectre that has been lingering on and haunting China for more than a century. The 'pain' it has caused could be felt constantly and regularly. The question for China now is: how far can Chinese higher education go under such a circumstance? Meanwhile, this makes China's case interesting to observe whether or not China could provide an alternative to the contemporarily dominant Western model.

Academic Culture

Another challenge for the Chinese higher education system is the academic culture. According to the Collins English Dictionary (1994), academic culture refers to the attitudes, values and beliefs that exist in higher education institutions. The attitudes, values and beliefs are held by academics in relation to all aspects of their professional work. A variety of highly related terms have also been used widely, such as "integrity", "ethics", "(mis)conducts", "(dis)honesty" and even "corruption". Higher education has its special standing in a society, and therefore a corrupt academic culture damages the standing of institutions and the academic community even more badly (Altbach, 2004b, 2005). Academic culture exists alongside the culture of the rest of the society. It includes among other things, the rules and regulations for appropriate behaviours on the part of teachers, administrators and students, as well as the philosophy that underlies teaching, learning, research and service at different levels. It is also about the beliefs held by those working within such academic institutions, such as a belief in original research and critical thinking.

As a set of attitudes, beliefs, and values that integrates a specific group of academics (Maassen, 1996, p. 158), academic culture has strong impact on what is done, how it is done, and who is involved in doing it, concerning decisions, actions, and communication on both instrumental and symbolic levels (Chaffee & Tierney, 1988). Altbach (2004a) has consistently cited it as a significant impediment for East Asian higher education to reach the leading status in the world. He uses terms including "academic life" (research, the distribution of research, the students, and the academic profession) (p. 14); "academic institutional traditions" (academic freedom, institutional autonomy, the relationship of the university to society) (p. 15); (indigenous) "intellectual and academic traditions", "academic model" and "the baggage of their historical past" (p. 18); and "shallow roots in the soil of their countries-the norms and values of academe" (p. 19). According to him, an academic culture that is based on meritocratic values, free inquiry, and competition is largely absent in East Asia (Altbach, 2010).

Since the 1990s in China, academic culture has fast become decadent and penetrated deeply into the higher education sector from regional to flagship institutions in almost every aspect of university operation (Ren, 2012). It has taken various forms including falsifying, plagiarizing academic achievements of others, obtaining scientific research projects or rewards by bribery and other illegal means, deliberately hiding academic scandals and covering up academic corruption by universities or research institutions. Those involved include students, professors, institutional leaders, and academicians (Yang, 2005). Within the Chinese system, performing research and holding an official capacity are closely linked. Academic performance has a direct bearing on advancement in administrative positions. Being promoted into the Government or even staying within universities with administrative positions can mean far more substantial financial reward than what pure academic work can bring. Chinese scholars are thus more and more prone to becoming trapped into the pursuit of administrative standing, rather than devoting their time to legitimate academic research.

China's academic culture portrays the wider society. Under the influence of *guanxi*, academic cronyism is widespread (Xiao, 2014). Free movement of staff, students and resources and career advancement of faculty is restricted. Decision-making is not based on academic merit, but personal relationships and preferential treatment. Plagiarism and the falsification of scientific results are common. Those in powerful positions carve up major research grants. Without many opportunities left for diligent individuals, academics seek instant success and quick profits only, and their acts of misconduct could be easily found in daily academic and administrative affairs. The toxic culture has devastating effects on higher education development and the entire nation's modernization, leading to distortion and inefficiency of institutions and the system.

It causes great damage to individual and institutional morale and to the style of academic work, ruins the academic atmosphere of Chinese universities and pollutes the mind of young students. It is serious enough to keep the development of China's advanced science from success (Guo, 2010). It has also affected the nation's ambitious deployment of the Chinese knowledge diaspora (Yang, 2005; Yi, 2010; Cai, 2012).

Comparing the fundamental cultural conflicts between Chinese and Western higher learning traditions, a rotten academic culture hurts the Chinese system more directly with evident impact on everyday operation. It is far beyond the higher education sector to solve such widely spread and deeply rooted social problems. With rampant academic dishonesty, it is fair to point out that China's State education policies began to stress the need for preventing research misconduct in the early 1990s. In 2006, the Ministry of Science and Technology and the Ministry of Education stepped up efforts in building academic norms and research integrity, through developing standards and regulations, setting up special agencies, issuing policy papers, organizing national forums or seminars, and promoting international cooperation. Some universities have launched their specific units to deal with academic fraud and corruption (Sun 2010). There are signs of clear awareness of such a serious issue within the Chinese higher education sector (Gong & Liu, 2013). It is also reasonable to expect some positive instantaneous policy effects. Yet, considering the general shortage of social trust and the width and depth of the issue within the society, it is just not realistic to hope that the problem would be uprooted within the coming years. This has also been confirmed repeatedly by my own research.

Conclusion

While Chinese universities have made tremendous strides in recent decades, the notion, which essentially aims at a judicious combination of Chinese and Western traditions as the fundamental mission of China's universities, has never materialized (Yang, 2013). Instead, China's promise is doomed to be limited (Altbach, 2010). Chinese universities have been able to improve their hardware considerably, while the software building takes much longer. Financial and other resources combined with some innovation strategies can make progress only so far. Simply buying state-of-the-art laboratory equipment will not guarantee the kind of intellectual atmosphere that has developed over centuries on European and American campuses. It is remarkable to see how China's strong traditions in higher learning have survived dramatic social and cultural changes in China's modern history, and remained deeply rooted among the Chinese people. Their impact on current higher education development is profound. They have been a negative asset so far. Only when their function is turned to be positive, can Chinese higher education lead the world, and only by then can claims about the Chinese model make real sense.

The bubbling and gurgling about China's rise in higher education in the English literature as well as in the media lacks a solid base. In the present great leap forward in Chinese higher education, what is often missing is sufficient attention to cultural and institutional establishments. Essentially, China's present higher education endeavour is part of its much more general process of seeking an alternative to Western globalization. Although integrating indigenous and Western ideas of the university is a must for the Chinese higher education system, it has never been achieved. Instead, the aforementioned two levels of challenges deal China's higher education weighty blows. Judged by the current practice and in consideration of China's deeply entrenched academic practices, China is likely to continue its path: learning the useful part while leaving the ideological aside. A handful of China's flagships will possibly join the distinguished leagues of the world's leading universities in scientific and technological research without much social and cultural influence at a global level. Chinese universities are not likely to challenge Western supremacy, especially because global university development is not a zero-sum game.

So far, very few people have been able to theorize how Chinese universities differ from their Western counterparts (Jaschik, 2011). However, it is important to note that nearly all the respondents in my recent research on China's top universities expressed their optimism about China's future success in building world-class universities (although some were more cautious than others). Despite that they differed substantially in their attitudes toward China's current situation especially in terms of academic corruption. Even those who strongly criticized China's academic culture were still optimistic about China's success in creating world-class universities. This contrasts sharply with the two extremes expressed in the English literature by international (indeed Anglo-Saxon) observers. It begs the question about the interaction between recognition and perspective and the difficulty of knowing anything in its entirety. Being able to watch the development of their institutions from within and based on their actual experience give much weight to the judgement of the respondents. It also urges us to reflect on the influence of 'Western' anxieties on perceptions of the changing geopolitical architecture of higher education located within an East-West binary which imagines Asia to be the West's 'other' (Bhabha, 1994).

References

Academic Ranking of World Universities (ARWU), Shanghai Jiao Tong University (2014). Academic ranking of world universities. Retrieved from *http://www.shanghairanking.com/ARWU2014.html.*

Altbach, P. (2001). The American academic model in comparative perspective. In P. Altbach, P. Gumport and B. Johnstone (eds.), *In defence of American higher education* (pp. 11–37). Baltimore, MD: Johns Hopkins University Press.

Altbach, P.G. (2004a). The past and future of Asian universities: Twenty-first century challenges. In P. G. Altbach & T. Umakoshi (Eds.), *Asian universities: Historical perspectives and contemporary challenges* (pp. 13–32). Baltimore: The Johns Hopkins University Press.

Altbach, P.G. (2004b). The question of corruption in academe. *International Higher Education, 34,* 8–10.

Altbach, P.G. (2005) Academic corruption: The continuing challenge. *International Higher Education, 38,* 5–6.

Altbach, P.G. (2010) The Asian higher education century? *International Higher Education, 59,* 3–5.

Ayers, W. (1971). *Chang Chih-tung and educational reform in China.* Cambridge, MA: Harvard University Press.

Bhabha, H. (1994). *The location of culture.* London: Routledge.

Cai, H.X. (2012). Deploying the Chinese knowledge diaspora: A case study of Peking University. *Asia Pacific Journal of Education,* 32 (3), 367–379.

Chaffee, E.E., & Tierney, W.G. (1988). *Collegiate culture and leadership strategies.* New York: American Council on Education and Macmillan.

Collins English Dictionary (1994). Glasgow: HarperCollins.

Gong, L.Y. and Liu, J.W. (2013). On academic culture and university soft power. *Academic Exchange, 6,* 216–219. (In Chinese)

Guo, J.X. (2010, June 2). Academic corruption undermining higher education: Yau Shing-tung. *China Daily.* Retrieved from *http://www.chinadaily.com.cn/hkedition/2010–06/02/content_9919871.htm*

Hartnett, R. (2011). *The Jixia Academy and the birth of higher learning in China: A comparison of fourth-century B.C. Chinese education with ancient Greece.* Lewiston, N.Y.: Edwin Mellen Press.

Hayhoe, R. (1989). China's universities and Western academic models. *Higher Education, 18* (1), 49–85.

Hayhoe, R. (1996). *China's universities 1895–1995: A century of cultural conflicts.* New York and London: Garland Publishing, Inc.

Hayhoe, R. (2001). Lesson from the Chinese academy. In R. Hayhoe & J. Pan (Eds.), *Knowledge across cultures: A contribution to dialogue among civilizations* (pp. 323–347).

Hong Kong: Comparative Education Research Centre, The University of Hong Kong.

Healey, N. (2012). Asia: The new powerhouse? ACA (Academic Cooperation Association) European Policy Seminar: Higher Education in 2030. Brussels, 12 October.

Jaschik, S. (2011, March 14). How Asian are Asian universities? *Inside Higher Ed.* Retrieved from *http://www.insidehighered.com/news/2011/03/14/asian_university_leaders_consider_identity_of_their_institutions.*

Kigotho, W. (2014, 28 February). China's rapid rise in global science and engineering. *World University News,* 309. Retrieved from *http://www.universityworldnews.com/article.php?story=20140227152409830.*

Kirby, W.C. (2012). The world of universities in modern China. *International Briefs for Higher Education Leaders, 1,* 4–5.

Knight, J. (2008). The internationalization of higher education: Are we on the right track? *Academic Matters: The Journal of Higher Education*, October/November, 5–9.

Knight, J. and de Wit, H. (1995). Strategies for internationalization of higher education: Historical and conceptual perspectives. In H. de Wit (Ed.), *Strategies for internationalization: A comparative study of Australia, Canada, Europe and the United States of America* (pp. 5–32). Amsterdam, The Netherlands: EAIE.

Levin, R. (2010). Top of the class: The rise of Asia's universities. *Foreign Affairs*, May/June, 63–75.

Li, J. (2012). World-class higher education and the emerging Chinese model of the university. *Prospect, 42* (3), 319–339.

Maassen, P. (1996). The concept of culture and higher education. *Tertiary Education and Management, 1* (2), 153–159.

Marginson, S. (2011). Higher education in East Asia and Singapore: Rise of the Confucian model. *Higher Education*, 61 (5), 587–611.

Ministry of Education (2014). National education statistics bulletin in 2013. Retrieved from *http://www.moe.gov.cn/publicfiles/business/htmlfiles/moe/moe_633/201407/171144.html.*

Mohrman, K. (2005). Sino-American educational exchange and the drive to create world-class universities. In C. Li (Ed.), *Bridging minds across the Pacific* (pp. 219–235). Lanham: Lexington Books.

Mora, J.G. (2001). Governance and management in the new university. *Tertiary Education and Management, 7*, 95–110.

Morgan, J. (2011, February 24). Sun sets on western dominance as East Asian Confucian model takes lead. *Times Higher Education*. Retrieved from *http://www.timeshighereducation.co.uk/news/sun-sets-on-western-dominance-as-east-asian-confucian-model-takes-lead/415300.article*

Morrison, J. (2014, February 6). China becomes world's third-largest producer of research articles. *Nature*. Retrieved from *http://www.nature.com/news/china-becomes-world-s-third-largest-producer-of-research-articles-1.14684.*

Postiglione, G. (2014). Research universities for national rejuvenation and global influence: China's search for a balanced model. *Higher Education*, published online 10 December 2014. DOI 10.1007/s10734–014–9838–6.

Ren, K. (2012). Fighting against academic corruption: A critique of recent policy developments in China. *Higher Education Policy, 25*, 19–38.

Sigurdson, J. (2004). China becoming a technological superpower-A narrow window of opportunity. East Asian Institute, National University of Singapore.

Sun, P. (2010). China's efforts for promoting research integrity. Professional Ethics Report 13, 4, 1–3.

Xiao, H.W. (2014). Chinese universities: Beware cronyism. *Nature,* 515, 492. Published online 26 November 2014, doi: 10.1038/515492d.

Yang, R. (2005). Corruption in China's higher education system: A malignant tumor. *International Higher Education, 39,* 18–20.

Yang, R. (2010). Much cry but little wool: Peking university personnel reforms. *International Higher Education, 60,* 10–11.

Yang, R. (2011). Self and the other in the Confucian cultural context: Implications of China's higher education development for comparative studies. *International Review of Education,* 57(3–4), 337–355.

Yang, R. (2013). Indigenising the Western concept of the university: Chinese experience. *Asia Pacific Education Review,* 14(1), 85–92.

Yi, L. (2010). Audit culture with Chinese characteristics? Returnee scholars' perception of Chinese higher education. Retrieved from *http://www.espacestemps.net/document8298.html.*

Zha, Q. (2011). Is there an emerging Chinese model of the university? In R. Hayhoe, J. Li, J. Lin and Q. Zha (Eds.), *Portraits of 21st century Chinese universities: In the move to mass higher education* (pp. 451–471). Hong Kong: Comparative Education Research Centre, The University of Hong Kong & Dordrecht: Springer.

Zhang, Y. (2009). *Western ideas of a university in China: Introduction and impact.* Hangzhou: Zhejiang University Press.

7

Ethnic Minorities, Integrative Nationalism and Higher Education in Yunnan Province

Ritu Agarwal

It has always been an uneasy exchange between the ethnic minorities in Western China and the Government of the PRC. Their strained relationships express two contending social perspectives. While the 'nationalities', as they are officially designated, hold more on to customary beliefs and practices, the Government wants them to embrace the modern economic and educational system introduced to them from outside. The integrative nationalism as these policies can be termed, has now completed a long circle from the initial autonomy promises, attempts at homogenizations and in recent years to more accommodative policy of recognition. But at the crux of these evolving policy paradigms is the Government's attempt to select, classify and accord ethnic minority or nationality status to these non-Han communities. Higher education proves to be a testing ground to evaluate the effectiveness and legitimacy of these policies and this paper attempts to examine whether the Government and the ethnic minorities are now evolving into a new set of exchanges where the Government secures its legitimacy in return for the cultural recognition of minorities.

There are fifty-five ethnic minority groups which are scattered across the regions of China. Though these are small in number they still constitute a significant part of China's population. Most of these minorities live in the frontier regions and their integration and control are considered necessary for the nation's development and stability. Thus, the cultural assimilation of non-Han people into Han culture was considered important and various practices like inter-marriages or State-led migration of Han population into these areas were adopted for this. Mao Zedong during the war against KMT and foreign imperialist forces reiterated that it will be to the benefit of minority population to be voluntarily attached with the central Chinese rule. The policies regarding the autonomy of ethnic minorities were codified in PRC's first Constitution in 1954 where Article 3, declared China to be single- multinational State of which the national autonomous areas are inalienable parts[1]. These autonomous areas largely referred to Tibet, Mongolia and Xinjiang. However, the goal of the CPC was to achieve the social, political and cultural equality between Han and non-Han population. The tensions between Han and non-Han population which existed in minorities-dominated areas were sought to be resolved by undertaking several measures like recruiting of local cadres into national leadership and respecting the special characteristics of the local population like their customs, languages and culture. However, there were incidences of conflict between the Han and the local population over the prevalent practices in these regions.

After Liberation, the special characteristics and particularities related to ethnic question were largely ignored. Inequalities based on religion, tribes and ethnicity were simply straight-jacketed under the socio-economic equality along the class lines. The national identification project of ethnic minorities was an important step to restore peace and stability in the country. An attempt was made to identify certain groups and thus create the conditions for their integration into a single nation. The ethnicity boundaries have been defined by the State without giving much consideration to their culture, tradition and religion. The market reforms were reformulated to enable these ethnic stereotypes to participate in the economic development process. Therefore, one could witness an assertion of ethnic identity through the revival of religion, culture and rituals in significant ways. This has often resulted in increasing tensions between the State and ethnic groups.

Various preferential policies like bilingual education, quotas in admission in higher educational institutions[2], etc. sought to integrate these ethnic minorities into the mainstream development discourse. As the statistics show, ethnic minorities gross access rate to higher education increased from 9.8 per cent in 1998 to 23 per cent in 2004. Still there has been a huge gap between Han Chinese and ethnic minority groups in terms of their access to higher education. Though the institutions of learning have increased and the number of ethnic minority students has also risen from the earlier percentages, the percentage of ethnic minority students enrolled in higher education is still below the percentage of minority population in these regions.

Another problem can be seen in the lower enrolment of these minorities in national level universities and much less in central universities like Beijing and Tsinghua Universities. Since 2000, ethnic minorities have accounted for 6.9 per cent of total number of undergraduate students each year at Beijing university. Tsinghua university enrols some 3,200 undergraduate students and among these only 200 come from minorities groups. Moreover, the minorities cannot make it to the most sought after courses like engineering, etc. They have to be satisfied with admission to liberal arts courses where there is not much competition. There are many factors responsible for the lower percentage of minorities in higher education. One important factor is the use and promotion of minority languages. Officially speaking, school education can be conducted in minority languages as permitted by legislation. The Chinese Constitution and relevant laws clearly guarantee the legal rights of minority groups to use and develop their own languages. In autonomous areas established for different ethnic minorities, local minority languages are official working languages in administration, elections, courts, broadcasting, publications and schools. However, for some minority groups, the scripts were developed by the Chinese Government, and in some cases are used in the early years of schooling before the transition to the Chinese script.

Moreover, in most of the minority autonomous areas, both the Mandarin and minority language are official languages. The Chinese Government established a parallel school system in autonomous areas in 1950. One is the ordinary school system, where Mandarin is a teaching language while English is a second language. Second, is a ethnic school system where local minority language is the medium of instruction while Mandarin is taught as a second language. Since Han people constitute a significant portion of the total population in many autonomous areas, Mandarin is used as a common language.

Besides there are other problems making the Government's efforts towards minority education including shortage of qualified minority teachers, non-availability of text books in minority language, lack of specialized ethnic schools, variations in preferential admission policies for the students, and the imposition of tuitions etc... work as inhibiting factors in promoting education in minority languages in ethnic areas.

One needs to further problematize this category as to ascertain who are these minority groups. What are the common linguistic and cultural characteristics they share? Are this categorizations based on common languages or do they share common religions and cultural characteristics? When did these ethnic groups come into existence and how do these groups relate themselves with the State? What have been the State policies regarding the revival of ethnic practices in China?

The paper examines two sets of themes. One, the State categorization of people into ethnic groups. It is necessary to analyse to as how the differences along the lines of religion, culture and language were simplified to establish political control in the border regions of China. It was particularly difficult as Yunnan was not integrated into mainland China and after the Liberation, the CPC took help of local elites, linguistics and central leaders to contain the diversity of interests within manageable limits. In this process, the State identification project has made some ethnic groups visible or others as non-existent. It is necessary to understand as to how these procedures made some groups even common and others different.

Secondly, it is to be examined whether or not the market reforms have challenged the existing boundaries or created the conditions for redefining ethnic boundaries in different ways. How do ethnic minorities negotiate with the State agenda of promoting economic modernization in these regions? How do these minorities transcend the State-defined boundaries of modernization by reviving its culture, religion and rituals? It is particularly evident in Yunnan as the region in the recent years has seen the revival of religious institutions like Buddhist temples, mosques and different cultural associations in significant ways. How do these religious institutions promote religious education as a part of ethnic revival strategies? Is this being regarded as a protest against State-designed educational agenda?

Yunnan, Ethnic Minorities and Classification Project

Yunnan presents an interesting model to study as ethnic minorities constitute a significant portion of population in the province. China has identified fifty-five ethnic minorities and among these, twenty-five can be found in Yunnan province itself. Some of these ethnic minorities include Bai, Dai, Yi, Miao, Buyi, Shui, Yao, Naxi, Hui, Hani, Zhuang, Jingpo, etc. Apart from these, there are minorities-inhabited autonomous prefectures as well like Dehong Dai and Jingpo 德宏 傣族 景颇, Nujiang lisu 怒江傈傈族, Diqing Zangzu 迪庆藏族, Dali Baizu 大理白族, Chuxiong Yizu 楚雄彝族, Honghe Hani and Yi 红河哈尼族彝族, Wenshan Zhuang and miao zu 文山壮族苗族, Xishuangbanna Daizu autonomous prefectures. 西双版纳傣族. These autonomous prefectures according to law have been given right to use their language, culture and religion and freedom to manage their political affairs.

Minzu is a very unique social category in China. *Min* in Chinese means people but it can also refer to a community, while *Zu* literally means human community groups. Officially minzu translates as nationality; more often it means ethnic groups. The term minzu for ethnic minority is very indigenous to China and each group has historically been established in particular regions. The ethnic minority groups as nationalities were recently defined by the State and many of these categories literally did not exist until their creation in 1950s (Jiaping Wu, 2012). In the official narratives of the PRC, the term ethnic minorities and nationalities are used as synonymous with each other. But they cannot be used interchangeably as there exists a marked difference between Minzu and Ethnicity. Minzu is a State construction, where ethnicity is being defined as a group with ethnic identity. While ethnicity is shifting and flexible, minzu is fixed and exclusive (Stevan Harrell, 1995). The ethnic status cannot be changed in one's life time and children from parents with different ethnicities can choose only one ethnic group as his or her lifelong ethnic group.

When the CPC came to power in 1949, it established its own political agenda. Its Constitution and the Common Programme after Liberation stipulated that China is a unitary, multi-ethnic nation-state. The Common Programme further stated in Article 50, *"All nationalities within the boundaries of the PRC are equal. They should establish unity and mutual aid among themselves and oppose imperialism and their own public enemies, so that the PRC will become a big fraternal and cooperative family composed of all its nationalities. Greater nationalism and Chauvinism should be opposed. Acts involving discrimination, oppression and disrupting the unity of the various nationalities shall be prohibited"*. It was further stated that because all nationalities in China have suffered from the oppression of foreign imperialism, all nationalities have to unite on an equal basis and make a joint effort in order to achieve national liberation. If any ethnic minority seceded from the motherland, it would certainly fall into being a colony of foreign imperialism.

After Liberation, CPC supposed itself to be the liberator and distributor of equal rights among previously exploited minority minzus. Under this ideology, it sought to control the frontier regions of China either through use of military power or by developing infrastructural links through these regions. It is especially true for the frontier regions where the ethnic minority population has more of trans-border linkages and considered crucially important for nation's development, stability and security. Another way of controlling the population in these areas was assigning the ethnic labels to them. It was especially the case in Yunnan where according to Yang Bin the main challenging task was to classify these ethnic groups into minzu category. As a result, the Government initiated the process of ethnic classification in early 1950s, firstly as to groups qualified officially to be a part of the minzu category. The process of ethnic classification was considered necessary to establish political control over this frontier region which was otherwise dominated by the so-called barbarian and uncivilized race.

It was in late 1949 and early 1950 that the Chinese State was able to establish its control over Southwest part of China which was mostly referred to as uncivilized because of large portions of minorities population, considered dangerous being a frontier region; therefore it was deemed necessary to integrate with the Chinese rule.

But the main problem was to manage the huge numbers of minority population residing in that region. To begin with, the State initiated the classification project to divide the ethnic population into various groups. Applications were invited from those who wanted to get the status of ethnic minority which essentially emphasizes the cultural differences from Han Chinese. It was estimated that there were almost four hundred applications received and the groups which shared common linguistic, cultural, geographic and economic characteristics were considered to be most qualified to get the minority status. In some cases for example, it was noticed that the ethnic minorities neither had a unified ethnic name nor common ethnic awareness before it was decided to put them into single ethnic group. This identification project which was partly created by the State was described by Dru C. Gladney as 'ethnic nationalism' which regard minorities as a group of people who share common cultures, common origins and ancestors.

The State used random criteria of family background, language, genealogy, and consanguinity as grounds for defining ethnic identity which is regarded as neither scientific nor objective in nature. The main question that arises here is what kind of groups can be officially designated as minzu. Han, Mongol, Hui, Manchus and Tibetans were already regarded as officially claimed minzu categories. Being a frontier region, it was difficult to identify the ethnic groups distinctly as there were many ethnic groups who lived within and across boundaries. To address this question, CPC dispatched a group of visiting delegations comprising provincial leaders and local elites to collect local social information. The main categories which were handy for putting ethnic population into various groups were their size, languages, history, their mode of living, education and cultural characteristics. After conducting surveys and case studies in villages, the information was compiled in a Draft of Collected Minzu Information in Yunnan in 1951. Still the problem was that there were many ethnic groups who lived near the border areas and it was difficult to ascertain their ethnic identities. (Bin Yang, 2009)

Even after Liberation, the administration of Yunnan Province especially in the frontier areas was still governed by the local chieftain system. As a result, the province was divided into two zones, one was an inland area where the ethnic population lived in compact groups, and the second was the frontier area. The State included places like Lijiang, Dehong, Xishuangbanna, Diqing, Linchang, Simao and Honghe altogether sixteen counties which were mostly located along boundaries in this frontier zone. The ethnic minorities like Dai, Hani, Zhang, Yi, Bai, Jiangbo, Lisu, Wa, Bulang, and Han which totalled a population of 2 million resided in the frontier region. It was designated as much problematic area where the identity of ethnic minorities was considered to be more fluid in nature.

It was in 1954 that the CPC Classification Project was finally launched. It was at this time that the investigations and identifications of ethnic groups were conducted on a much larger scale. To carry out this huge ethnological project, the Central Minzu Affairs Commission was set up as the main institutional body. Later, visits were undertaken to areas like Wenshan, Mengzi, Yuxi, Lijiang, Dali, to study Yi, Zhuang, Dai, and Hani ethnic groups. Besides scholars, various other institutions like United Front Department of Yunnan Party Branch, Minzu Affairs Council, Institute of Language, Yunnan University, Yunnan Minzu College, were involved. Altogether there were 68 ethnic units identified. Yi, Bai, Dai, Miao, Hui, Wa, Hani, Lisu, Naxi, Jingpo, Zang, Yao were identified as the important minzu categories. Other categories were of those who were considered to be the branches of existing Minzu. Language played an important role in designating a group as minzu. There are over eighty languages used among these ethnic groups. The ethnic groups which have their language and a written script as Mongols, Tibetans, Uyghur, Kazak, Kirghiz, Korean, Yi, Lahu, Jingpo, Xibo were easily granted the minority status. For the groups which have a spoken language but not a common written script, the Chinese writing system was commonly used.. Moreover, the groups which had smaller populations and were scattered around were put under one category. For some minority groups like Zhuang, Yi, Buli, Miao, Dong, Hani, Lsu, Li Wa and Naxi, the Chinese Government created written scripts and even adjusted writing characters for Dai, Lahu and Jiangpo and designed new scripts for Uyghur and Kazak.

The local government played a pioneering role in the identification of minzu in Yunnan. The main institution which was set up for ethnic identification was Minzu Affairs Office in 1951 at the government and the Party level in Yunnan. The main task of Provincial Minzu Affairs Commission was to find out the composition of ethnic minorities, i.e. their population, social and cultural characteristics and it thus left enough space for manipulation.

Officially twenty-five ethnic minorities were identified as minzus which were Yi, Bai, Hani, Zhuang,, Dai, Miao, Jiangpo, Lisu, Hui, Lagu, Wa, Naxi, Yao, Zang, Bulang, Pumi, Nu Ancahng, Deang, Jino, Shui, Man, Menggu, Buyi and Dulkong in Yunnan Province. In 1987, the state announced that the project was basically completed. But the problem was of those who could not be placed into any group or those who were not happy with their ethnic minority status. So, the problem was to identify those who were unidentified and to re-identify others who were unsatisfied with these ethnic units.

The identification project has left both negative and positive legacies. Sometimes, it has placed the small and disadvantaged groups of population into ethnic or sub-ethnic groups which had positive implications for that group. It was through this process that many ethnic minorities became conscious of their ethnic identity. Sometimes, the classification of many minorities group into one single unit helped to create common consciousness. It has often resulted especially since 1980s in the emergence of ethnic nationalism posited by Gladney that subsequently engendered challenges to the State authority.

While the majority accepted their categories, the classification proved to be problematic. While 56 minzus have been created along over 400 applications, many other ethnic or sub-ethnic groups have been forgotten. Henry G. Schwarz argued that minzu lacks a clear definition and that minzu identification lacks a clear standard. The local government units which played an important role in designating some groups as minzu often made this classification on arbitrary grounds.

In cases, where ethnic and administrative boundaries overlap each other, there was further misrepresentation of ethnic identity. Moreover, the lack of co-operation among other local government across these administrative boundaries often led to misclassification.

Thirdly, tension among the ethnic units further added to this problem. The groups which were dominant were assumed as minzu without any prior investigation or research. In Yunnan itself, there were 13 ethnic units which were regarded as minzu because they had been publicly acknowledged for a long time. The relation with local elites and party officials made some groups as relatively dominant. It has largely affected their own classification and also of the neighbouring ethnic people.

The minzu identification in China only fashioned the identity of these groups and in a way was a continuation of the imperial legacy. It was an organized top-down State project. Minzu Shibie or ethnic classification can be seen as an attempt by the State to render eligible the diverse groups of people living within the country. The ethnic identification project has been criticized as an attempt to determine the position of a particular group in the ladder of hierarchy on the basis of the deemed status at the time of the communist take-over. It has not fully respected the wishes of the common people as to whether they want to be associated with a particular ethnic group or not.

Religious Revival and Minorities Education in Yunnan

The relations between State and ethnic minorities in China have undergone serious contestations and negotiations over the years. There have been a series of ethnic conflicts between Han and Uyghurs in Guangdong and in Urumqi in Xinjiang and then clashes between Han and Tibetans in Lhasa. Many studies have cited the economic deprivation as one of the important reasons as the State has followed the preferential policies of favouring coastal regions over others. In the process of homogenization of the development discourse, most often many of these communities have been forced to leave their traditional places which were rich in natural resources and avenues of traditional knowledge. The marketization process has affected their livelihood options and thus made them marginalized in these regions. The State development policies are very much in question as these are detrimental to local culture and the sustenance of the knowledge system of the region. It has resulted in various forms of ethnic violence, demand for autonomy and assertion of ethnic identity.

As a response to these ethnic conflicts, the State has initiated some policies in favour of minorities like quotas in educational institutions, tax exemption and revival of ethnic religion, cultural institutions and values. One of the important steps in this direction has been the admission quotas in higher educational institutions and introduction of bilingual education at the university level in China. These education policies for minorities require universities to relax their admission standards to an appropriate extent for minorities.

Preferential admission is facilitated by several factors. One element is to make the process of taking the national entrance examination easier for minority students by allowing them in many cases to use indigenous language. Minority students who seek admission to 13 nationalities universities and to some of the 117 minority area universities can become *min kao min* (minorities taking the examination in minority language). They can attend minority area universities rather than schools in larger Han coastal areas. But the minority students who are from ethnic groups without written language like Li, Bai or who live in areas where the minority population is linguistically diverse find it difficult to retain their local language.

Another factor which presents a challenge to State policies on education is the revival of religious education especially among some of the ethnic minorities in Yunnan Province. There has been as assertion of religious identities in terms of revival of rituals, values and cultural practices associated traditionally with ethnic minorities groups. It is clearly reflected in the increase in the number of Buddhist monasteries and the places of religious practices like temples and mosques in the region. It has been particularly noticed in case of some minorities like Bai, Dai and Hui in Yunnan Province. In many parts, the opening-up of religious schools associated with these Buddhist temples and mosques indicate an alternative mode of education than the one supported by the State through the preferential policies in quotas in admission in higher education institutions. The question arises as to whether this revival of religious practices and assertion of ethnic education indicate a challenge to the cultural cohesion practices of the State. Are these ethnic minorities associating themselves with different forms of organizations than the one propagated by the Chinese State? Does this indicate non-assimilative or pro-separatist tendencies among these groups? Does the revival of minorities' cultural practices present a new form of resistance to the State-unifying agenda of assimilating the minorities into one single nation?

The study by Susan Mccarthy on 'Communist Multiculturalism' explains that the State responses to the assertion of ethnic identities have been quite positive. Considering the increasing number of tensions between Han and minorities or among different ethnic minorities, State has made a shift from its earlier approach of being assimilative to one towards being more accommodative to this plurality of interests. This has largely been noticed in the promotion of their religion, art and culture of ethnic minorities as a part of maintaining their traditional life styles; however, the State still follows the national identity which is essentially Han-centric.

In this context, the study of the Dai minority is quite important as it constitutes over 1.3 million of the total population and they are quite distinct in their linguistic, religious and other cultural practices which set them apart from mainstream Chinese Han society. The State has conspicuously promoted Dai culture and religion in Xishuangbanna which is a Dai minority inhabited region. The place has the potential of an important commercial centre under Yunnan's regional co-operation of the Great Mekong River Project and thus it can become an important gateway city to its borders in Thailand, Laos and Myanmar. Dai's art, customs, culture, dance, architecture and music have been vigorously promoted by the State. Dai culture has been used as an instrument to promote tourism in the region and attract economic investment.

Dai was a highly stratified minority who strongly followed the Buddhist principles and values. It has been argued that Buddhism especially Theravada Buddhist practices were quite popular in Xishuangbanna which is essentially a Dai minority inhabited region. The religious practices are so prevalent that every village has a temple which was a centre of religious, social and educational activity. Broadly speaking, these temples were the main network centres of religion and the political power emanates from here. Even the written language of Dai is composed of Sutras and scriptures of Buddhism. In case of Dai being located mainly at the border of the region, the distinctiveness of ethnic culture is difficult to challenge and they still show their reluctance to get integrated into Han mainstream dominant discourse. It is quite visible in the revival of these Buddhist institutions after the reforms. The most visible example of this is the renaissance of Theravada Buddhism which has long been central to Dai life. It is particularly important as traditional Dai Buddhist education of monks is considered to be in direct opposition to the state education. The increase in the number of drop-outs among novitiates from the state-run schools suggests that Buddhist temple schools are seen by many Dai people as a viable alternative to State education. While Buddhist temple schools are seen as a viable alternative to State education by many, there are others who still regard State education as a necessary and valuable tool for modernization. Though Chinese officials look at Buddhist education with scepticism and as backward, they still support religious revival. Dai on the one hand are supposed to participate in the State modernizing agenda clearly visible in promotion of tourism industry in the region and it is also needed to maintain the traditions and customs which define them as minority. Through State promotion of Dai art and culture, Dai have often been portrayed as backward and exotic. Dai enjoy the reputation of a model minority as they are perceived as a docile community.

In comparison with Dai, the integration into Han culture was rather easier in the case of Bai minority nationality. Culturally and politically, Bai was not such a politically conscious ethnic identity as was Dai. Bai Minority people reside almost entirely in Yunnan in Dali Bai autonomous prefectures. Bai used to be regarded as an 'Imagined Community'. Prior to mid-1950s, Bai people rarely referred to themselves as ethnic, and instead they called themselves as minjia, Fitzgerald considered the minjia to be a distinct ethnic group, mainly on the basis of their language. Their sense of minority or ethnic identity was a weak one. But by the minority classification of 1950s, local officials regarded the worship of the local deity (Benzhu) as the proof of Bai distinctiveness. Bai has often been regarded as unique in the sense it is open to adoption of Han cultural values and has been integrated well with diverse people and practices. There have been a good number of institutions promoting bilingual education. The opening of bilingual education in both Chinese and the local scripts indicate the integration of this minority well into the Chinese culture. Bai are well represented among faculties of colleges and universities throughout the province and nationally. Bai is considered to be comparatively advanced in relation to other minorities. Most of the works characterizing Bai as a distinct identity were destroyed during fifteenth century and the Bai written system has been devised in consonance with Mandarin phonetic language. Even bilingual education in Dali has suffered setbacks due to practical and resource constraints.

The party-state has given birth to this imagined community that is Bai; for example Bai written language was created. Through the creation of a minority nationality, a sense of collective nationhood was generated. Since Bai was already considered to be more advanced than other minorities, there was not any need felt to maintain its distinct identity through a different language.

Hui is one minority which is scattered all over China and religion is an important marker of their ethnic identity. Hui are indistinguishable from the Han and other minority groups. They share a language, an economy and general cultural practices but do not share a common territory. Their degree of integration with the Han varies by region. However, still considered to be possessing a strong self-identity and they have been often called as 'familiar strangers'. Religious resurgence in terms of rebuilding of mosques and establishing Islamic schools have revitalized their religious networks and community life. Though the revival has created conditions for asserting the rights and privileges of ethnic minorities, there are differences of opinion regarding the purpose of revival, its meaning, traditions and formulations of Chinese Islam that should be promoted. Some have embraced a Wahabi-influenced Islam that encourages detachment from secular and non-muslim society that surrounds them. Other Hui support the reconstitution of an existence and identity that is as Chinese as it is Islamic. (McCarthy, Susan K., 2009). These competing perceptions of Islamic identity complicate further Hui people's drive for legitimacy and modernization. The revival of various holidays and festivals of Hui communities indicate the opportunities for the assertion of ethnic identity. The rituals like Ramadan give this community an opportunity to establish transnational linkages with other Islamic groups beyond the boundaries of village, township, county and even prefecture.

The Islamic education as argued most often does not set any standard curriculum and is left to the interpretations of religious leaders. Islamic education and Arabic education is seen by some as ignoring the history of Yunnan Hui Muslims. Hui seems to possess a historical and cultural Chineseness which seems to be more integrating with Han. Thus, the combination of Islamic and Han culture seems to give rise to this nationality. If they have adopted Han *wenhua* or Han culture well, they are considered to be advanced Minzu. It was quite evident as the spread of Islamic and Arabic only education is considered not just a rejection of modernization but also a repudiation of genuine Hui identity and tradition. In fact, in the case of this particular ethnic minority, the market reforms have started the process of de-ethnicization and the revival of religious identities make them more integrated with trans-local religious boundaries. This entire process in a way challenges the ethnic identities which were essentially State-defined.

The State has sought to achieve twin objectives through the process of cultural revival. It has accepted that there is the need to maintain diverse ethnic identities as they are reflected in promotion of minority art, culture and religion. However, it has also emphasized that their integration into mainstream development through bilingual education for example will redefine their ethnic identity as being modern. The cultural revival among Dai, Bai and Hui minorities in Yunnan really complicates the process of integrating them with Han modernization discourse on the one hand and maintaining their ethnic differences on the other.

The questions of higher education seem to be different in these minorities region as there is also a need felt by the ethnic communities to revive the education along the lines of their culture and religion which has long been suppressed over the years. The conflict between the State-run educational institutions and minority religious education does not seem to come into much contradiction as the registration of these institutions require the State approval. The modernizing discourse of the Chinese State seems to integrate well the minority communities. The Dai, Bai and Hui ethnic revival in a way redefines national goals and ideals that make them modern, minority and Chinese.

Interestingly, Yunnan, though is the home to more than a dozen ethnic minorities, has not seen a kind of unrest which often explodes in Xinjiang and Tibet. Though it will be wrong to say that the province is without any ethnic tension, still the State has been able to integrate ethnic minorities into the modernization drive and has also created the conditions for maintaining the ethnic differences. The revival of religious and cultural values and institutions also depends on the location of a particular group geographically and also its linkages with national and transnational factors. The linkages of these minorities with other groups across borders and the nation may make them assertive about their identity; however, they have to depend on the State for the articulation of their folklore, traditions and values. The State mainly in Yunnan seems to modernize these ethnic people especially of Bai, Daị and Hui through integrating them with the market economy. However the State has also emphasized the need to maintain their ethnic distinctiveness. They seem to be integrated well only through their unique lifestyles, traditions and culture which in a way legitimizes the State presence in these minorities-dominated areas.

Notes

1. Article 3 of the Chinese Constitution adopted in 1954 lays down: The PRC is a unitary multinational state. All the nationalities are equal. Discrimination against or oppression of any nationality and acts which undermine the unity of nationalities are prohibited. All nationalities have the freedom to use and develop their own spoken and written languages and preserve or reform their own customs and ways.
2. This national policy is well reflected in section 65 of the 1984 Law on Ethnic Regional Autonomy as:
   The state shall set up institutions of nationalities, and in other institutions of higher education, nationality oriented classes and preparatory classes that enrol only students from minorities nationalities. Preferred enrolment and preferred assignment of jobs may also be introduced. In enrolment, institutions of higher education and secondary technical schools shall appropriately set lower standards and requirements for the admission of students from minorities nationalities.

References

Bin Yang, 'Central State, Local Governments, Ethnic Groups and the Minzu Identification in Yunnan' (1950–1980s), *Modern Asian Studies*, Vol. 43, Issue 03, May 2009.

Colin Mackerras, *China's Minorities : Integration and Modernization in the twentieth Century*, Hong Kong: Oxford University Press, 1994.

Dru C. Gladney, *Muslim Chinese: Ethnic Nationalism in the People's Republic*, Cambridge: Council on East Asian Studies, Harvard University, 1991.

____ 'Ethnicity, Local Interests and the state: Yi Communities in Southwest China', *Comparative study of Society and History* 32(3) 1990.

Stevan Harrell (ed.) *Cultural Encounters on China's Ethnic Frontiers*, Seattle and London: University of Washington Press, 1995.

Susan K. McCarthy, *Communist Multiculturalism: Ethnic Revival in Southwest China*, Seattle and London; University of Washington Press, 2009.

Thomas Heberer, *China and Its National Minorities: Autonomy or Assimilation?* Armonk & New York: M.E. Sharpe, Inc, 1989.

Xiaolin Guo, *State and Ethnicity in China's Southwest*, Leiden: Boston, 2008.

8

Sweden's Contribution to Human Rights Education in China and the Raoul Wallenberg Institute

Anamika

The Tiananmen incident turned a watershed in the history of the relationship between China and Europe. Post-Tiananmen, the issue of Human Rights (HR) has become a defining feature of all the events, foreign policies, and discussions involving China and Europe. Realizing the fact that China is a powerful economic player in the world market, and hence unavoidable in many ways, Sweden in association with the European Union (EU) initiated a long-term dialogue with China. This dialogue was around the issues of sustainable development, poverty alleviation, gender equality and HR. This discourse has involved various agencies, institutes, NGOs and universities of Sweden and their counterparts in China paving the path for sustainable development, decrease in poverty, gender parity along with upholding the internationally recognized HR.

The struggles over human rights pose opportunities and threats to political stability, economic development, and international peace (Shun 2007: 151). Keeping this in focus, the Government of China turned the HR issue into an opportunity than a threat to its international relations. The pragmatic Chinese Government agreed to take infrastructural, financial and academic support from Sweden to address the issue of HR in the late 1990s. At this time, all the three Nordic countries,

Sweden, Norway, and Denmark initiated HR training and capacity build-up programmes in various universities and legal institutions in China with the help of their HR centres, such as the Raoul Wallenberg Institute for Human Rights and Humanitarian Law (RWI), the Norwegian Centre for Human Rights (NCHR), and the Danish Institute of Human Rights (DIHR). This paper attempts to explore and assess the role of Sweden in promoting Human Rights Education (HRE) initiatives in China, focusing on the intervention of Raoul Wallenberg Institute, the challenges it faced during 2000–12, and the implications of these interactions for the future discourse on human rights education promotion in China.

What is Human Rights Education (HRE)?

The Universal Declaration on Human Rights (UDHR) paved the way for initiating the project of HRE in the signatory countries. China is one of the signatories and is hence liable to initiate and take forward the mission of HRE. HRE is all encompassing in nature. HRE addresses the developmental aspects of an individual in totality. Human rights education provides important means to raise the awareness of citizens and promote the implementation of human rights (Xia 2013: 723). In 2009, China came up with a National Human Rights Action Plan of China (NHRAPC) which was extended and currently the 2012–15 Action Plan is in progress. The Action Plan is a bold step in reiterating the commitment of China to recognize and promote international HR. The NHRAPC is meant to cover all aspects of international HR. (Smith and Bai 2012) argue that Action Plan is a milestone in creating a culture of human rights education. The culture of human rights cannot simply be imposed from above or through international conventions, but must be grounded in everyday life experiences and struggles (Svensson 2006: 123). The Action Plan spreads over the educational levels from primary to higher. The Action Plan has five sections covering areas of economic, social and cultural rights to civil and political rights to the rights of ethnic minorities, women, children, elderly people and the differently-abled to education in human rights to exchange and cooperation in the field of international human rights. In this paper, the focal point is section 4, sub-section 36 that deals with education in human rights in institutes of higher learning. The following quote from NHRAPA (2009–12) explains the Government's position as well as the policy on HRE:

> The state continues to encourage institutions of higher learning to conduct research and education in human rights theory. Investigations into human rights education will be conducted in a number of institutions of higher learning, while scholars from universities and colleges are encouraged to carry out human rights studies. The state will promote the formulating of plans for human rights education in institutions of higher learning, encouraging them to offer human rights as an elective course to all undergraduate students, and offer the course of human rights law to undergraduate students majoring in the science of law. It will promote the compiling of textbooks on human rights law and the development of teaching courseware. A number of institutions of higher learning which started human rights education earlier than others will be designated as the bases for human rights education and training (NHRAPC 2009–12).

The Action Plan intended to promote HR research and education in human rights theory at higher educational levels in China. It faced challenges and had some obvious limitations. Keeping in mind that HR education and research had just begun in China, courses offered in HR became elective. There was a lack of trained teachers in HR. The scarcity of human resources in HR made the course optional both for teachers (in terms of offering an HR course) and students (in terms of choosing an HR course). Finally, there was a dearth of literature on HR in Chinese. The limitation of resources thus slowed down the pace of HRE in China. Meanwhile, the UN Declaration on Human Rights Education and Training (UNHRET) came in 2011. By incorporating the provision of HRE in the NHRAPC, the Chinese Government had already laid the foundation for HRE prior to UNHRET-2011. It was not therefore difficult for China to adhere to the declaration and show commitment to promote HRE at all levels of education. Article 2 of the UNHRET-2011 defined HRE as follows:

> Human rights education and training comprises all educational, training, information, awareness-raising and learning activities aimed at promoting universal respect for and observance of all human rights and fundamental freedoms and thus contributing, inter alia, to the prevention of human rights violations and abuses by providing persons with knowledge, skills and understanding and developing their attitudes and behaviours, to empower them to contribute to the building and promotion of a universal culture of human rights (Article 2, UN Declaration on Human Rights Education and Training 2011).

The above definition found a place in the Action Plan too. The Action Plan vowed that HRE would be spread at all levels through various modes including formal educational institutions and media, both print and electronic. The State was engaging its apparatus to increase awareness about HR amongst its people. But the most challenging part for China would be to create a human rights culture that permeates throughout the Chinese society.

China's Position on Cooperation in Human Rights Education with European Countries

After Tiananmen, the Western world severed its relationship, albeit briefly, with China over violation of the right of the people for peaceful demonstration. With the resurgence of China, the West soon desired to reestablish contact with it. Bjornstol wrote that in the mid-1990s, the human rights discourse between China and the Western countries became less confrontational with more focus on diplomacy and dialogue (2009: 3). China also realised the importance of amicable relationship with the outside world for its economic expansion and returns. In this backdrop, the China Foundation for Human Rights Development (CFHRD) was established in 1994 with the objective of improving HR conditions in China and collaborating with foreign countries on the issue of promotion of international HR (CFHRD's website). It received sufficient funding for the publicity, promotion and training in HRE (CFHRD's website). The Foundation was also entrusted with the responsibility of overseeing the implementation of National Human Rights Action Plan. Section 5, clause 2 of the Action Plan that has been devoted to international exchange in HR laid out a plan for the Government to cooperate in the field of international HR with other countries. The provision for international exchange in HR was first stipulated in NHRAPC, 2009 and reiterated in 2012:

> China is committed to holding exchanges and cooperation in the field of international human rights on the basis of equality and mutual respect. China continues to hold dialogues and exchanges on human rights with various countries on the basis of equality and mutual respect. China also increases consultation and cooperation on human rights with developing countries (NHRAPC, 2012–15).

The provision prepared a policy ground for international exchange in international HR. This further strengthened the already existing relationships with the Nordic countries that began in 2001. In the following sections, we shall examine how China used HR to promote cordial relationships especially with the Nordic countries.

Raoul Wallenberg Institute and Human Rights Education in China

Raoul Wallenberg Institute of Human Rights and Humanitarian Law was instituted in 1984 at the Lund University, Sweden. The institute was established to promote research, training and academic education in the area of human rights and humanitarian law (RWI Report No. 19: 7). Keeping the objective and ongoing work of RWI in sight, the Swedish International Development Authority (SIDA) assigned the responsibility of evolving a programme of HRE for developing countries to the institute in 1990 (Ibid.: 8). In addition to that, RWI has also started collaborating on the issue of HRE with Nordic countries such as Denmark, Finland, and Norway. The outcome of these two developments resulted in the introduction of HRE in China since early 2000. The RWI programme of HRE in China has three components: academic, justice and legal aid to NGOs (Anger and Bergling 2008: 9).

This paper addresses only the academic component of HR project of RWI in China. The academic component sought to strengthen the international HR law in Chinese universities through establishing Master's Programmes, developing literature, research, training, and arranging workshops for faculty members (Ibid.: 9). RWI has also offered a few short and long term scholarships and fellowships for the Chinese students and faculty members to go to Sweden and experience the nature and dynamics of HRE practised there.

Collaboration Between Chinese Universities and RWI

The RWI has been involved in the promotion of HRE in China since 1996 but mostly in an informal capacity. In 2001, the RWI opened its Beijing office. To initiate its first academic collaboration, RWI signed a memorandum of understanding with the Peking University's Law School (PULS) and helped them in setting up a Master's Programme in HR (leading to a certificate awarded by Peking University and RWI after completion of the course) in 2004. There are twenty-five seats in the human rights Master's Programme. The duration is of two semesters and the eligible students are all the enrolled candidates in Master's and PhD programmes at Peking University. The objectives of the collaboration with PULS are to "establish a cadre of professionals skilled to work institutionally and individually for the promotion of human rights (based on international standards and principles); improve the institutionalisation of human rights education in China; and provide a model for similar initiatives at other universities." (Ibid.:12)

The objectives indicate that RWI intended to intensify its presence in the field of HRE in China by establishing collaborations with other universities. The objectives are also suggestive that RWI is only addressing the international HR standards and principles. In addition, adherence to international HR standards and principles would provide a model of HRE for other universities as well. All said, questions can be raised about the extent to which the RWI model of HRE could lead to complete institutionalization of HR in China. Institutionalization implies HR becoming an integral part of the functioning of the various political, economic and cultural systems of the country. This has to be predominantly from below, rather than from above. The impression one gets from the RWI's objectives of HRE is more of a top down approach. The course structure of HR programme at PULS reinforces the impression. The course consists of the following papers: "Human Rights and the Rule of Law (compulsory); International Mechanisms for Human Rights Protection (compulsory); International Humanitarian Law (optional); Series of Lectures in Human Rights Protection (compulsory); Civil, Cultural, Economic, Political and Social Rights (compulsory); Regional Protection of Human Rights (optional); Minority Rights protection (optional); Business and Human Rights (optional) (Ibid.: 15)."

A close examination of the courses does not fully convince that institutionalization of HR can be achieved through this course structure as the course structure is essentially focused on legal aspects of international human rights. It does not give an opportunity to the students to connect international human rights with the social, cultural, and local realities of China.

> Human rights education and training comprises all educational, training, information, awareness-raising and learning activities aimed at promoting universal respect for and observance of all human rights and fundamental freedoms and thus contributing, inter alia, to the prevention of human rights violations and abuses by providing persons with knowledge, skills and understanding and developing

their attitudes and behaviours, to empower them to contribute to the building and promotion of a universal culture of human rights (UNDHRET, 2011).

It is clear from the above quote that the programme can however create a common understanding about international HR standards and principles among those who are taking up these courses. But it cannot become instrumental in institutionalizing the HR culture in China. The scope of the programme is also limited in the sense that it is open only to Peking University's post-graduate and doctoral students. Hence, the reach of the programme and its outcome are extremely limited.

Since 2004, the RWI has also been helping the China University of Political Science and Law (CUPSL) in building the capacity of its faculty members, researchers, and students. The CUPSL with the RWI has jointly organized a series of four lectures on HR between 2008 and 2012, five HR law summer school programmes (2009–13), and two workshops on justice and HR protection in 2011 (Ban 2014). However, the role of the RWI is limited as these programmes are of short terms and the nature of involvement of the institute is merely supportive. It is not in a position to engage in a long-term relationship and hence be involved in university level decision making on the issue of HRE.

Exchange and Fellowship Programmes of RWI

International exposure adds to the understanding of HR. HR are universal but every country tends to explain them creatively in a certain local context. Hence, international exchange becomes an essential feature of HRE in broadening its scope. In the context of China, international exchange in HRE turns out be far more crucial since Chinese teachers, researchers and students may interpret HR in ways that are substantially different from the Western definition. Sensing the value of international exposure in international HR studies, the RWI made provisions for Chinese educators, scholars and students to visit the institute in Lund. It also offered fellowships with provisions to travel to other European countries and experience their international HR studies programmes. Sun argues that with the knowledge acquired abroad, the RWI sponsored scholars are playing active and significant roles in promoting human rights education and research in China (2006: 69).

The Lund University in collaboration with the RWI started a Master's Programme in International Human Rights Law at the Faculty of Law almost two decades ago. The course is one of its kind as it has both the theory and praxis components that make it an effective international human rights law programme. It is also designed in a way to cater to the needs of both the local and foreign students. The RWI offers two scholarships to Chinese students to do a Master's in International Human Rights Law at the Lund University. After the completion of the course, the students are expected to go back and work in their area of interest and promote the cause of HR in China.

The RWI in collaboration with PULS has also been sponsoring internships abroad of Chinese students enrolled in the Master's Programme in Human Rights running at the PULS. These include a six months' internship for two interns at the Irish Human Rights and Equality Commission, and a one month's or two weeks' internship for six students at the Hong Kong Asian Human Rights Commission (Law Department, PKU). The opportunities for short-term internship outside China, though limited, have proved quite useful in offering differing perspectives on the functioning of international HR. The young Chinese interns gain an edge over others in terms of knowledge and skills acquired from their foreign internships and they are more capable of contributing to the discourse on international HR.

The history of teaching and research in international HR in China goes back to the mid 1990s. Prior to that, not many teachers and researchers were involved in HR studies. The researches conducted by the Chinese scholars in the field of human rights are stated to be politically motivated (Sun 2006: 70). Researches, not many, were essentially aimed at justifying China's position on HR. One of the objectives of the RWI in Beijing is capacity building in international human rights. The capacity building programme includes training of teachers both in China and at the RWI, Lund. The programme has also a provision for fellowships for Chinese teachers to do research at the RWI. These fellowships range from three to six months of full sponsorship by the RWI. Chinese scholars have utilized research facilities and resources of RWI, and attended programmes, conferences, and workshops on HR. Most of them have acquired basic training in international human rights in China arranged by the RWI's Beijing office. Initially, in these training programmes, Swedish HR experts were invited to orient the Chinese. In the second phase, Chinese scholars were sent to Sweden to enrich and sharpen their knowledge and hone their skills. Once back from Sweden, many of these scholars offered an elective course on international human rights. They accepted that the RWI programme had helped them immensely in teaching courses in international human rights programme at the Peking University (Yeh, 2008). The training on home turf and foreign exposure gave them confidence to offer a course in HR which was highly unlikely earlier.

Human Rights Literature and RWI

For the successful implementation of HRE, it is mandatory to have sufficient reading and research material. In the beginning, at least, there has to be a set of good textbooks to introduce the concept of HR to the students. The case of China is peculiar, as many Chinese students prefer to read in Mandarin that further complicates the ready availability of relevant material. The RWI, therefore, had to deal with three issues in order to increase the number of students signing up for the courses in HR: arranging sufficient reading material on international human rights, providing standard textbooks on human rights in simple English, and last, but not the least, to initiate the process of translation of available standard material on international human rights into Mandarin. In the mid 1990s, China showed keen interest in the project of HRE but the State was not ready to invest in it financially. The inability of the Chinese Government to invest in the project of HRE meant that it now became RWI's sole responsibility to bear the expenses incurred on promotion of HR including the development of scholarly literature on international human rights and make it available to the universities and institutes involved in teaching and research.

Literature Acquisition Project

The RWI with financial assistance from SIDA initiated its Literature Acquisition Project (LAP) in 1992 covering twenty institutions in fourteen countries. The aim of LAP is spelled out below:

> The literature acquisition project aims at facilitating access to books, journals, articles, reports,, etc. on human rights-relevant topics for researchers, teachers, students, and other "key" groups in resource-poor countries and regions. It is expected that these materials will serve as a basis for further education, training and research activities in the field of human rights, and otherwise help the institutions and "users" promote and protect various aspects of human rights in the respective countries. Indeed, the project has helped to generate a number of publications, spurred debate and improved awareness, and helped to increase the respect for critical aspects of human rights and rule of law generally. It is also widely appreciated among the participating institutions and other bodies concerned with human rights issues in the respective countries (Collins-Falk and Bergling, 2003: 2).

The biggest challenge for the developing countries in promoting HRE is investment in HR literature as economic returns are negligible. In the absence of HR literature, any meaningful propagation of HR is not possible. This has been the reasoning behind RWI's initiative to provide HR literature to the developing countries. To avail this facility, a country has to apply and after getting selected, it is entitled to acquire approximately fifty titles per year from a standard list of reading material. The process of selection of countries for this is rather simple and the RWI routinely accepts almost all the applications (ibid). China has been one of the beneficiaries of this project. The number of Chinese libraries with a section on the gifted books from the RWI is gradually increasing. Yeh (2008) stated that the Chinese libraries found the RWI gifted material on HR very useful for the students of all courses and disciplines as the readings included mostly basic literature on HR.

Translation of HR Literature into Mandarin

There is a significant increase in the number of Chinese students and scholars who can read and write in English. But when it comes to preference, they tend to choose Mandarin over English. It was discovered at the RWI that the LAP initiative is not delivering the desired results as there are not many takers for the HR literature in English. To address this issue, the RWI in collaboration with the NCHR funded a project focused on translating standard HR literature into Mandarin. The translation of major international declarations, treaties, and covenants, such as UDHR, International Covenant on Economic, Social and Cultural Rights (ICESCR), International Covenant on Civil and Political Rights (ICCPR) were done in the first stage. Sun (2006) has provided the names of the first three books published in Chinese: "The Universal Declaration of Human Rights: A Common Standard of Achievement edited by Gudmundur Alfredsson and Asbjørn Eide; Economic, Social and Cultural Rights: A Textbook edited by Asbjørn Eide, Catarina Krause and Allan Rosas; and U.N. Covenant on Civil and Political Rights: CCPR Commentary by Manfred Nowak (p. 72)."

The translation of international documents on HR into mandarin was an important effort of the RWI but once again not quite adequate as many Chinese scholars questioned the quality of the translations. To address the issue of standards in translation the RWI commissioned the writing of textbooks on HR in Mandarin from 2002 onwards. The Chinese education system places particular emphasis on the use of theory in all disciplines. There was a challenge faced by the HR textbook writers to amalgamate the reading material on HR with theoretical grounding. The RWI invited Chinese scholars to discuss the production of a standard textbook on HR in Chinese, but nothing came out of it. Meanwhile, the RWI is helping in developing the PULS's online courses on HR.

The RWI is also engaged in training activities comprising an annual Advanced Workshop on International Human Rights Law for University Teachers, a seminar on multidisciplinary human rights research methods and an introductory human rights course for university teachers (SIDA Report 2008: 12).

Promotion of HRE in China: Challenges Faced by RWI

Woodman (2007) in her study on the role played by international NGOs (INGOs) in promoting the knowledge of international HR found that there has been a trust deficit between China and the INGOs (pp. 135–136). This is true to some extent as the RWI Report (2002–23) explains as to how workshops conducted by the institute were videotaped for scrutiny. The RWI has been involved in the HRE project in China for over a decade now but the presence of the institute is still restricted to the PULS. The institute aimed at institutional capacity building in international HR in China. For it to be fully successful, the RWI ought to be meaningfully present in a significant number of universities, colleges, and research institutes.

For the promotion of HR culture in a society, it is imperative for HRE to permeate all disciplines from primary to higher education. As Svensson argued, it should be part of daily life experiences (2006). This implies that people of China should know and experience that their HR are being respected on a daily basis. The biggest challenge in front of the RWI is to expand the scope of its capacity building from legal or law education to other disciplines because the knowledge of HR *capacity-building-programme-in-china-2004–2007_1936.pdf.* (accessed on December 25, 2014).

Ban, Wenzhan. 2014. 'Foreign Exchange and Cooperation in Human Rights Education: A Case Study of the China University of Political Science and Law', *Human Rights*, Vol. 13, No. 1, January. *http://www.chinahumanrights.org/CSHRS/Magazine/Text/t20140416_1166817.htm.* (accessed on February 19, 2015).

Bjornstol, Elisabeth P. 2009. 'Human Rights Law Education in China', *Web Journal of Current Legal Issues*, Vol. 1, *http://webjcli.ncl.ac.uk/2009/issue1/pdf/bjornstol1.pdf.* (accessed on May 22, 2015).

Colling-Falk, Anna and Bergling, Per. 2003. *The Raoul Wallenberg Institute's Literature Acquisition Project. www.rwi.lu.se/pdf/evaluations/lap.pdf.* (accessed on June 30, 2015).

Li, Baodong. 2006. 'Human Rights Education in China' in Jonas Grimheden and Rolf Ring (eds), *Human Rights Law: From Dissemination to Application-Essays in Honour of Göran Melander.* Leiden and Boston: Martinus Nijhoff Publishers, 47–56.

National Human Rights Action Plan of China. 2009. *http://www.china.org.cn/archive/2009–04/13/content_17595407.htm.* (accessed on January 16, 2015).

National Human Rights Action Plan of China. 2012. *http://news.xinhuanet.com/english/china/2012–06/11/c_131645029.htm* (accessed on November 24, 2014).

Raoul Wallenberg Institute of Human Rights and Humanitarian Law Report No. 19. 1994. *Raoul Wallenberg Institute 1984–1994: The First Ten Years.* Sweden: University of Lund.

Sida Country Report 2007. 2008. *http://www.sida.se/contentassets/1bff5bf1c8c84092838b6f086c05f210/china_505.pdf.* (accessed on 28 June 2015).

Smith, Rhona and Bai, Guimei. 2012. 'Creating a Culture of Human Rights Education in China', (on-line festschrift in honour of Katarina Tomaševski). *http://rwi.lu.se/wp-content/uploads/2012/04/Human-Rights-Education-in-China-Smith-and-Bai.pdf.* (accessed on October 28, 2014).

Sun, Shiyan. 2006. 'Human Rights Education and Research in China: The Contribution of the Raoul Wallenberg Institute' in Jonas Grimheden and Rolf Ring (eds), *Human Rights Law: From Dissemination to Application-Essays in Honour of Göran Melander.* Leiden and Boston: Martinus Nijhoff Publishers, 57–84.

Sun, Zhe. 2007. 'Normative Compliance and Hard Bargaining: INGOs and China's Response to International Human Rights Criticism' in Baniel A. Bell and Jean-Marc Coicaud (eds), *Ethics in Action: The Ethical Challenges of International Human Rights Nongovernmental Organizations.* Cabbridge: Cambridge University Press, 151–168.

should not be restricted to a single discipline, no matter ho significant. The RWI is addressing the issue of language b appointing staff and hiring researchers equipped with Chines linguistic skills but the pace at which these human resourc are yielding results in terms producing research material i Chinese is slow.

Conclusion

From the above discussion, it can be argued that the RW has played a significant role in the promotion of internation human rights education in China. It was RWI that broke th deadlock in communication between China and the outsid world in the mid 1990s. It is credited with the initiation of constructive dialogue with the Chinese State without offendin the host country's sensibilities. The RWI throughout adopte a cautious approach keeping in mind the high possibilit of China getting annoyed. It always maintained a dignifie relationship with the Chinese Government. The RWI is on the first INGOs that opened their offices in Beijing with th Government's best wishes and support. It invested heavil in the area of promotion of international human rights, b introducing a course, building capacity while training teache through workshops, seminars and sponsoring them to g abroad one could get first hand experience in international HI Though the progress of RWI's programmes and initiatives slow, there can be little doubt that they are going to continu working in China for a long period of time. The Chines teachers, scholars, researchers and students have spoke positively about RWI's HRE initiative in China. If China an the RWI could bridge the trust deficit, the initiatives will gai in speed and prove successful.

References

Anger, Joakim and Bergling, Per. 2008. *Review of Raoul Wallenbe Institute's Human Rights Capacity Building Programme in Chin* 2004–2007. *http://www.sida.se/contentassets/059c0afda8eb42008e9df 96709fa34/200823–review-of-raoul-wallenberg-institutes-human-right*

Svensson, Marina. 2006. 'Beyond Culture: Rights Talk and Activism in China' in Edmund Ryden SJ and Barbara K. Bundy (eds), *Human Rights in the Pacific Rim: Imagining a New Critical Discourse.*

Taiwan: Socio-Cultural Research Centre, Fujen Catholic University, 109–138.

United Nation as Declaration on Human Rights Education and Training. 2011. *http://www.ohchr.org/EN/Issues/Education/Training/Compilation/Pages/UnitedNationsDeclarationonHumanRightsEducationandTraining(2011).aspx.* (accessed on 20 January 2015).

United Nations Declaration on Human Rights Education and Training. 2011. *http://www.ohchr.org/EN/Issues/Education/Training/Compilation/Pages/UnitedNationsDeclarationonHumanRightsEducationandTraining(2011).aspx.* (accessed on May 20, 2015).

Woodman, Sophia. 2007. 'Driving without a Map: Implementing Legal Projects in China Aimed at Improving Human Rights' in Baniel A. Bell and Jean-Marc Coicaud (eds), *Ethics in Action: The Ethical Challenges of International Human Rights Nongovernmental Organizations*. Cambridge: Cambridge University Press, 132–150.

Xia, Yongmei. 2013. 'Analysis and Suggestions for Improvement of Human Rights Education in China' in 2nd *International Conference on Science and Social Research,* 720–723. *www.atlantis-press.com/php/download_paper.php?id=7816.* (accessed on November 23, 2014).

Yeh, Jessica I. 2008. 'Promoting Human rights in China through Education: An Empirical Impact Evaluation of the Swedish Approach from Student Perspectives'. *blog.hawaii.edu/aplpj/files/2011/11/APLPJ_10.1_yeh.pdf.* (accessed on December 25, 2014).

Notes on Contributors

Anamika was formerly a faculty at the Central Institute of Education, University of Delhi. A PhD from National Chengchi University, Taiwan, she is a recipient of Taiwan Government Scholarship, AusAId Grant, GeorgEckert Fellowship among others.

Ritu Agarwal is Associate Professor at the Centre for East Asian Studies, School of International Studies, Jawaharlal Nehru University, New Delhi. A PhD from the University of Delhi, she has studied at the Beijing Language and Culture University. Her research interest is Yunnan Province and she has been affiliated to the Yunnan Academy of Social Sciences, Jinan University, Guangzhou, Chinese University of Hong Kong and National University of Singapore.

G. Balatchandirane is Associate Professor, Department of East Asian Studies, University of Delhi where he teaches Japanese Economics. He has been a visiting Faculty at Kanazawa University and Yokohma University both in Japan. His publications include: *Gender Discrimination in Education and Economic Development: A Study of Asia, Tales Diaries Tell: Agriculture and Historiography in Pre-war Japan* and *The Roving Indian and Stagnant Japan.*

Sreemati Chakrabarti is a former Professor of Chinese Studies, Department of East Asian Studies, University of Delhi and Vice-Chairperson, Institute of Chinese Studies, Delhi. Her earlier publications include *China and the Naxalites, Mao, China's*

Intellectuals and the Cultural Revolution, Taiwan Today (Edited with Anita Sharma) and a document for the National Book Trust of India titled *China*.

Ka Yin Chau is the Executive Associate Dean of the Faculty of International Tourism and Management, City University of Macau.

Saumen Chattopadhyay is Professor at the Zakir Hussain Centre for Educational Studies, School of Social Sciences, Jawaharlal Nehru University. His book *Education and Economics: Disciplinary Evolution and Policy Discourse* was published by Oxford University Press. His other publications include works on Black Economy, fiscal issues and higher education research.

Shiyan Lou is an Associate Professor at the City University of Macao. She obtained her doctoral degree in applied economics and her field of research is human capital theory and economics of education.

Aishna Sharma is a doctoral student at the Zakir Hussain Centre for Educational Studies, Jawaharlal Nehru University. Her area of interest includes education policy analysis, governance issues in higher education and globalization and higher education.

Kavita A. Sharma is President, South Asia University. She has been Director, India International Centre and Principal, Hindu College, University of Delhi. Among her publications are *Internationalization of Higher Education in India: An Aspect of India's Foreign Policy*.

Yang Rui is Professor and Associate Dean for Cross-Border International Engagement in the Faculty of Education at the University of Hong Kong. Bridging the theoretical thrust of comparative education and the applied nature of international education his research interests include educational policy, comparative cross-cultural studies in education, international higher education, educational development in Chinese societies, and international politics in educational research.

Rui Yang is Professor and Associate Dean for Cross-Border International Engagement in the Faculty of Education at the University of Hong Kong. Bridging the theoretical thrust of comparative education and the applied nature of international education his research interests include educational policy, comparative cross-cultural studies in education, international higher education, educational development in Chinese societies, and international politics in educational research.